LISTENING FOR THE VOICE

ENDORSEMENTS

"Twenty years ago, Roger Nelson was challenged to stay in one place and see what would be created by his words. The sermons contained in these pages are the fruit of that challenge, evidence that Roger's words matter and make a difference. The people of Hope Christian Reformed Church know first-hand the creative power of these words. They also know that without love, even the most eloquent words, whether spoken by humans or angels, are nothing more than a noisy gong or clanging cymbal. What can be intuited from this collection is something the people of Hope already know: that for twenty years one has come among them and spoken the truth, the Word of God, with love."

– JEFF MUNROE

editor of *The Reformed Journal* and author of *Reading Buechner*

"A preacher who can write (or maybe he's a writer who can preach), Roger Nelson has humbly wrestled with Scripture for 20 years alongside a faithful congregation just outside of Chicago. It's a gift that a number of his sermons—along with reflections on his time in the pulpit—are now more widely available. For those who live in hope, more so on some days than others, these are sustaining words."

– JOSH LARSEN

author of *Movies Are Prayers: How Films Voice Our Deepest Longings* and *Fear Not! A Christian Appreciation of Horror Movies*

"I know preachers who never find their center of gravity because they're so busy acting and role-playing. Roger Nelson never joined that club. His honesty is refreshing, his ministry moves are truly authentic, and his words in this little book sing."

— PETER W. MARTY

editor/publisher of *The Christian Century*

"Roger has a unique and rare ability to be faithful to the text while relating it to our existential realities. Drawing on his own life, popular culture, and connecting the text to human vulnerability, Roger brings a much-needed authenticity. This collection of reflections and sermons is a wonderful gift in very anxious times."

— DAVID OLSEN, PhD

Executive Director of Samaritan Counseling Center of the Capital Region and co-author of *Saying No to Say Yes: Everyday Boundaries and Pastoral Excellence*

LISTENING FOR THE VOICE

COLLECTED SERMONS & REFLECTIONS ON PREACHING

ROGER NELSON

BROKEN SPOKE BOOKS

LISTENING FOR THE VOICE

ISBN 979-8-218-19590-8

Published by Broken Spoke Books
2246 Marston Lane, Flossmoor, IL 60422

Design by Schuyler Roozeboom

writing for the wobbly wheel

For Sandi

"I've got reservations about so many things, but not about you."

— JEFF TWEEDY

CONTENTS

INTRODUCTION

I took it as guidance from God. The voice was a rumply-tweedy professor, but I took it as guidance from God.

In the late nineties and early aughts I was serving as a youth pastor at First Reformed Church of Schenectady, New York, and enrolled in the Doctor of Ministry program at Princeton Theological Seminary. I had no idea what I was doing. The work at the church was neither challenging nor satisfying, and I thought the Princeton degree would lead to new opportunities. But mostly I was lost – wandering about and going through the motions.

As a restless and remarkably mediocre student in college and seminary, I spent time lurking in the shadows, floundering in class, and sitting in the back row of lectures. I was envious of my classmates' chummy confidence as they chatted over coffee with professors.

> Therefore, when I started at Princeton, I vowed to change my ways. I wanted to study with vigor, find a mentor, and come to a modicum of vocational clarity. That seems like a lot to ask of a part-time professional certificate program…

The transformation that I hoped for didn't happen. While I made friends, I did the bare minimum of classwork, kept my distance from professors, and muddled my way toward the thesis paper. The expectation for graduation was that students would do original groundbreaking research that would be of service to the church universal. These final projects were shaped by rigorous reading lists and a specific research model. I was happy to read, but I couldn't figure out how to fit my existential questions into the research expectations.

So, floundering and frustrated, I finally took a deep breath and knocked on Dr. Jack Stewart's office door.

Dr. Stewart was a church history professor who'd served a long, successful pastorate and was an advisor for the Doctor of Ministry program. I can't remember any other professors' names, and I'm sure none knew mine, but Dr. Stewart was an affable fellow. I didn't know where else to turn; I went to him to inquire about my options.

Dr. Stewart welcomed me with a warm smile, cleared academic clutter off a chair, and set aside his pipe. He couldn't have been kinder, but when I began to voice my struggle, he got up and closed the door. Returning to his desk chair, he squared himself, looked me full in the face, and said,

> *This program is a mess. We all know it. But you don't need this degree. It doesn't mean a thing in your polity* (church governance). *We've had our eyes on you. You're an arty guy. You need to plant yourself in a church and preach for 20 years and see what difference it makes.*

I have no idea what was said next or how our meeting wrapped up. The only thing I remember is walking out of his office and watching Princeton University soccer practice. Dr. Stewart didn't know that I was working with a therapist and wrestling with life in ministry. Neither did he know that I was approaching an intersection without a clue about which way to go. I was stunned by what he said, and all I can recall now is sitting on the bleachers in the sun – mystified.

As it turns out, two roads diverged, and I took the one Dr. Stewart pointed toward. I took it as guidance from God.

Within a few weeks I returned a call to Hope Christian Reformed Church, and within a few months we were moving from north New York to south Chicago. I dropped out of Princeton and accepted the call to be Hope's pastor.

The actual decision was far more complex, and I surely don't know if God directs our lives in that manner. The work I was doing with a therapist was weighty, my longing for Chicago was strong, and all sorts of other issues were jostling in my heart. As a husband and father, uprooting felt risky. Accepting a call to be a pastor felt riskier. But that conversation with Dr. Stewart set me on a 20-year journey, and the Princeton program gave me exactly what I needed.

However, I never finished Dr. Stewart's directions.

He told me to see what difference preaching makes. And while that difference may simply be that I had something to do for 20 years, I'm inclined to finish the task. If it was guidance from God, I should probably see it through. This little writing project is an attempt to fulfill that assignment. After planting myself in a church and preaching for 20 years I want to think about what I've learned.

After this introduction, there's a series of sermons that were spoken in Hope.

> Years ago, a faithful Hope member – with the beard of an Old Testament prophet – encouraged me to do something similar to this project, saying, "We need examples of work faithfully done." Therefore, what follows is not a collection of greatest hits but examples of the weekly work of wrestling with scripture. I trimmed them down for this format, but they're emblematic of theme, voice, form, question, and biblical genre. They're neither the best nor the worst. I hope they read as work faithfully done.

After the sermons there are reflections on what I've learned. Maybe 20 years of preaching counts as a research model. Maybe this gets at the existential questions I couldn't make fit…

The last thing the world needs is one more book about God. This is not an attempt to break new theological ground. I have no misgivings about my voice or my limitations. Anything I have to say is derivative. These are the reflections of a restless practitioner. I'm just trying to finish what I started. I'm trying to give an accounting of what I did for the last couple decades.

A couple caveats…

Preaching is a spoken art – these sermons were written to be spoken. There's something lost in translation from voice to page. If you've been listening over the years, you'll probably hear me in your head. If you've stumbled on this project, I hope something of the preaching moment is communicated in the reading moment.

Preaching is umbilically tied to scripture. I'd encourage you to read the sermons before reading the reflections. I'd encourage you to read the biblical texts before reading the sermons. I'm grateful for you reading any of this, but the sermons are rooted in scripture. Start there.

You will notice that the formatting is odd. I don't do it to be hip or artsy. It's the way that I write. Breaking things up on the page helps me preach rather than read. There's no organizational science or grammatical rules. I can only attest that it's how I hear or see the rhythm of preaching.

And finally,

I'm grateful for the grace that the people of Hope gave me as a preacher.
I'm grateful for their patience.
I'm grateful that they kept showing up.
I'm grateful that they let me hang around for so long.
I'm grateful for the sabbatical to work on this little project.
This is one way that I can say "thank you" to those that "gather in Hope."

ROGER NELSON
March 2023

SERMONS

Changing God

GENESIS 9:8–17

Hope's high school youth group, affectionately known as Yeeps, went to Rehoboth, New Mexico, to do demolition in preparation for the construction of a new school building. With a joyful vibe, about twenty of us did a week of hard labor and accomplished far more than the organizers thought possible. Towards the end of our stay the Rehoboth leaders offered to show us the landscape and living conditions of the Native American reservation.

We piled into a short bus. Without enough seats, I stood on the front steps and talked to the bus driver. He was our crew boss. He talked about the good work and good spirit of our group – wishing that all groups were like our group.

As we drove and talked, he asked how we survived with all those liberal churches up there where we came from. I asked what he meant, and he referenced churches that ordain women as elders, deacons, and preachers.

> Bewilderment washed over his face when I told him we were one of those churches. Stunned. This revelation boggled, buffaloed, and blew up his worldview. He was not supposed to like us…

When he recovered, he started to talk about the desert, the rock formations, and the environment. At one point he told me that fossils from sea creatures had been found in these stone hills, providing proof of the flood in Genesis.

Bewilderment washed over my face. He believed God flooded the whole earth and wiped away every person – save the few on the ark – because the Bible told him so and the proof was fossilized in the hills of New Mexico.

Dear friends, what are we to make of the story of Noah's ark?
How might we read it?
Rather than relegate it to children's storybooks and the interpretations of Hollywood, what can we learn from it?
How can it set us on this Lenten journey toward the cross and empty tomb?

You remember the story. God looks down and is anguished by the wickedness of humanity. Seeing the corruption and brutality, he regrets that he made man and woman in the first place and resolves to,

> *...wipe mankind, whom I have created, from the face of the earth.*

However, you might be surprised to learn that there is actually no mention of anger or wrath or fury. The language is that God is grieved. The heart of God is broken by the heart of humanity. And God's cry is to,

> *...put an end to all people, for the earth is filled with violence because of them.*

God's heart breaks because of the violence. So, from *shalom* to chaos, from garden to sewer, God's ready to flush the whole mess.

Scott Hoezee frames it this way:

> *Tragedy and pathos fill these chapters. So does an unspeakable amount of death. We may have grown up liking the image of all those animals tucked safely into the ark, but there's a reason no children's storybook has ever shown dead animals and dead people floating all over the place on the floodwaters. I don't know what to make of that part of the story. Seeing God in the light of grief over against seeing God as a ruthless dispenser of divine fury helps to soften things quite a bit, but it does not remove the scandal of the cataclysm depicted here. This is finally a hard story to grasp.*

This is a hard story to grasp. And yet, what if it's a story not about creation changing but about God changing?

God sees and spares Noah.
In some ways Noah is the new Adam.

> He "embodies a new possibility" (Brueggemann) for humanity. The heart of God was grieved, so he wiped the slate clean and began again with Noah. This is a do-over. And therefore, when Noah and his boys and their assorted wives finally climb down the gangplank onto dry ground, they build an altar.

Take that image at face value: The land would be littered with dead, bloated, water-logged bodies. The decomposing carcasses of animals and people alike would be stinking to high heaven. And in the midst of that odor of death, Noah burns an offering of thanksgiving and its aroma is pleasing to God. Then scripture records that God said in his heart,

> *Never again will I curse the ground because of man, even though every inclination of his heart is evil from childhood. And never again will I destroy all living creatures, as I have done.*

The post-flood world may still be a stinking mess, but God now promises restraint. These lines are almost identical to what God said when announcing the coming deluge, but rather than promise destruction he now promises to sustain creation. Humanity hasn't changed, but God has changed.

In 1976 The Alan Parsons Project released their debut album, *Songs of Mystery and Interpretation*. Their music was grandiose and dramatic and it included a version of the Edgar Allen Poe poem about a perched raven pecking out an unchangeable promise. The chorus is a rocking version of,

> *Thus quote the Raven, "Nevermore. Nevermore. Never.*
> *Nevermore. Nevermore. Never..."*

Dear friends, God's heart, broken by creation, is changed to make covenant with creation. God goes from grief to promise, from judgment to assurance. And the promise that God makes is, "Never again." Grandiose and dramatic is the voice of an unchangeable covenant, "Never again. Never again. Never again..."

No matter how bad things get, the lid may blow off and all hell break loose, there may be holocaust and horror, war and the rumors of war, the violent shadow of the human heart may cast its darkest, but "never again" will God destroy by flood – an ancient symbol of mythological chaos. The posture of God's heart has changed from indictment to covenant.

Scott Hoezee is helpful here:

> *The flood narrative situates God between grief and grace. Both grief and grace are responses to human sin but at the end, grace speaks the last, best word. God is not going to stop being offended and grieved by sin, of course. But from now on, God says grace is going to lead the way. God is going to find a way to see our sin yet without destroying us in that sin. God will find a way, in other words, to forgive. God will find a way, to quote the New Testament, to bring about a new truth: "While we were yet sinners, God loved us and saved us."*

I'm not sure that this story is about Noah's faithfulness in building a boat when there wasn't a cloud in the sky. Nor is it about the miracle of fitting all the animals "two by twosy" on the "arky, arky."

Neither is it a warning shot of God's judgment upon sin. (If you thought the flood was bad, wait until you see the fire.) And I doubt that it's about how all humanity came from the loins of Noah and his boys when the boat finally ran aground on top of a mountain – in New Mexico.

But the story of Noah is about the changed heart of God and the possibility of a changed human heart. The sign of that change is a rainbow. God places a rainbow in the sky not just to remind us of his promise but to remind himself. Reaching high over creation, like a rainbow, there is the promise that God won't destroy.

> It's a covenant with all creation – it includes the creatures and the critters. It's a multigenerational covenant – it includes Noah and his brood, and all those who would come after. It's a covenant of hope – God's fundamental orientation toward creation is one of mercy, not retribution. It's a covenant of memory – God will see and remember. We will see and remember.

As we begin our journey toward the cross, the ground we traverse, is the promise of God. May we remember in sign and symbol – even in this bread broken and this wine poured out. And may that foundational promise cause us to walk with a clear-eyed confidence in the heart of God, a confidence that led singer-songwriter John Calvin to write:

Our hope is in no other save in Thee;
Our faith is built upon thy promise free;
Lord, give us peace, and make us calm and sure,
That in thy strength we evermore endure.

Amen.

Via Chicago

GENESIS 12:1–5

On a late summer night, with a hint of autumn at the edges, my daughter and I caught the train to see Wilco at Pritzker Pavilion in Millennium Park.

As the sky went dark, the skyline lit up, and all the colors of the city were mashed together on the brushed metallic shapes soaring above the stage. The sound was exquisite, the sky was cloudless, the air was crisp, the show was sold out, and the crowd was trendy-cool and self-absorbed. With my high-school-aged-daughter beside me – texting a boy and tolerating my musical tastes – life felt rich and full and good. Abundant.

Wilco is a scruffy Chicago-based rock band fronted by Jeff Tweedy. They play a sort of alternative-Americana-dissonant-white-guy-dad-rock. (That's a genre.) I've lost track of how many times I've seen them…

Midway through the show Wilco began a song with a gentle melody that rose to a cataclysmic climax and then fell away to a barely voiced whisper:

Searching for home, searching for home, searching for

> *home, via Chicago, I'm coming home, I'm coming home, I'm coming home, via Chicago...*

And, hushed and holy, the crowd of 11,000 sang along.

I'm not a hand raiser in church, but my hands went up and tears of deep thanksgiving pooled in my eyes from the sheer beauty of it all. My daughter, the music, and the night were overwhelmingly grace-full – as a crowd of young professionals sang of their search for home...

Maybe that reads too much into the lyrics and the moment, but it felt like a hymn-sing for those trying to find healthy, honest relationships,
a sense of purpose,
authentic community,
something bigger than our selfish impulses,
and a place to belong.

In a word, it was a mighty chorus of people longing for *shalom*.

Biblically understood, *shalom* is more than a feeling and far more than the absence of conflict. *Shalom* can be defined as,

> *...universal flourishing, wholeness, and delight – a rich state of affairs in which natural needs are satisfied and natural gifts fruitfully employed, all under the arch of God's love.*

On a summer evening between the lake and the towered-city-of-man it felt like we were singing of our longing for *shalom*.

Searching for home, searching for home, searching for home via Chicago...

Dear friends, we clearly don't live in *shalom*.

We live in a world where young men with military weapons kill students in classrooms, families at parades, and old women at church. We live in a world where creation's resources are plundered, where the scales of an equitable economy are out of whack, where war terrorizes, and where the arch of God's love can seem missing, muted, or marred. We live in a world that is often marked by fear, alienation, and death.

Scripture tells the story of *shalom*'s spoilage.

In Genesis 2 we're kicked out of the garden and reminded that all will surely die; in Genesis 4 brother has murdered brother; by Genesis 6 violence has filled the world until God floods the whole the mess; and by Genesis 11 we're building towers to make a name for ourselves. So, in Genesis 12 God breaks in and calls Abram.

One way to read God's call of Abram is that as the world careened into chaos, God broke in to establish a covenant through which all creation would be blessed and God's way of *shalom* would be restored. In the words of Walter Brueggemann:

> *The purpose of the call is to fashion an alternative community in a creation gone awry, to embody in human history the power of the blessing. It is the hope of God that in this new family all human history can be brought into the unity and harmony intended by the one who calls.*

That's to say that in the call of Abram, there's a call to blessing, a call to *shalom*, a call back home.

Slow Man, by South African Noble laureate JM Coetzee, tells the story of an old bachelor who loses a leg in a bicycle accident. The novel is about loss, aging, and finding self. At one point, while talking about home, the old man says:

> *Hearth and home, say the English. To them, home is the place where the fire burns in the hearth, where you come to warm yourself. The place where you will not be left out in the cold.... Among the French, as you know, there is no home. Among the French to be at home is to be among ourselves, among our kind...*

I don't know if that's true about the English and the French, but it's a helpful distinction: home as place or home as people.

It's easy to read the call of Abram as the call to a place,

> *Go to the land I will show you...*

It's just as easy to read it as the call to a people,

> *I will make you into a great nation...*

Home as place.
Home as people.
But, what if God's call to Abram is not primarily about place or people? What if those are only avenues to the blessing that God desires for all creation?

In a world marked by fear, alienation, and death, God calls Abram and Sarai to be a channel of blessing for all people. Place and people are only the ways in which God breaks in to restore right relationship,

to restore belonging,
to restore *shalom*.

What's lost in our text this morning is that Abram was the last branch of a family tree. His father was dead, one brother was dead and the other brother was left behind, so all Abram had to offer was his broken-down old body and the barren womb of his wife. And yet, God chose Sarai and Abram.

He didn't choose Ham or Shem,
Nahor or Nimrod,
Siskel or Ebert,
Calvin or Hobbs.
God chose Abram.

Maybe God's point is that humanity is at a dead end. In the natural process of begetting and begatting, in the unfolding of generations, in being fruitful and multiplying, God picks Sarai and Abram precisely because they're an ending.

They're powerless to fix a future.
They're hopeless to make a family.
They can't conjure up or create a thing.
They can't even imagine anything different.
The best they can offer is barrenness.

In the words of Walter Brueggemann,

Barrenness is the way of human history.

But God breaks in and says:

> *I'll make a way – you follow.*
> *I'll lead you home – you trust.*
> *I'll restore shalom – you be a blessing to others.*

Dear friends, does that read too much into this text?

As those with a deep longing for *shalom* in our bellies, for a people with the memory of the garden fixed in our imaginations, for a people imprinted with the image of God, for a people who are metaphorically barren, is it plausible that God would break in and make covenant with a wandering Aramaean for the sake of creation's *shalom*?

Does God break in to lead us home?

We moved three times when I was growing up. As a child I lived near two major universities and one small liberal arts college. Those childhood moves left me wondering where I came from and to whom I belonged. Was home a place or a people?

In my early twenties, an internship landed me in Chicago, and in some ways I've never left. I found a home, both a place and a people. I sang along with Wilco on the lakefront because it was my story:

> *Searching for home, searching for home, searching for home, via Chicago. I'm coming home, I'm coming home, I'm coming home, via Chicago…*

But now in my early sixties, maybe I've learned that home is never fully a place or a people but the avenues by which we can be a blessing to others. Maybe home is about how we use our gifts for the good of others. Maybe home is joining in God's pursuit of *shalom*.

One way to read scripture is as God's relentless search to restore *shalom*.

I hesitate to use the language of God "searching." As if he can't find it. But there is an unfolding quality to the story of God and creation. God creates, commands, seeks, calls, and promises to get to the *shalom* for which creation was intended.

That search for *shalom* makes its way through Christ, the cross, and the resurrection. And that search for *shalom* is ultimately about God breaking in to call me and you.

I don't know what you brought with you this morning:

Maybe your broken-down-old-body, maybe your barrenness, maybe a weary soul searching for home, maybe thanksgiving, maybe indifference? Maybe a deep longing to join a chorus singing for *shalom*…

The good news, dear friends, is that God keeps breaking in and calling us to be blessing for others. God continues to call us as agents of *shalom* in our families, in our friendships, in our neighborhoods, in our world…

The way of *shalom* is the way of reconciliation, forgiveness, servanthood, death, and resurrection. Ours is simply a matter of following the call of God, following the way of Jesus.

You are called to *shalom*.
You are blessed to be blessing.

Until we all join together in singing in a mighty chorus…

> *I'm coming home, I'm coming home, I'm coming home, via Chicago…*

Amen.

Shining Stars

GENESIS 15

It happened again. A paunchy-naked-old-guy decided that the gym shower was an appropriate place to ask a question about church.

He started by asking why I wasn't doing a Wednesday night service. I told him that while we did Ash Wednesday, the midweek service was not a tradition of the congregation I served. Undeterred, even as I turned my face back into the shower, he continued, "What ever happened to the Dutch Reformed Church?"

"Well," I told him, "there really isn't a Dutch Reformed Church. There are two branches of the Reformed tradition in America with Dutch roots: the Reformed Church in America and the Christian Reformed Church of North America."

His eyes glazed over. This was not what he wanted to hear. He responded, "No, the Dutch Reformed! When I was a kid, they couldn't dance or play cards. They had to wear long pants; they couldn't do anything on Sundays. What happened to them?"

As I toweled off, I told him I didn't know anything about all that, and he turned toward some other bloke in the shower and started talking about his tomato plants.

But it did get me to wondering: How are Reformed folks defined? What's distinctive about the Reformed tradition? When people think about us, what commitments or characteristics come to mind? Are we defined by rules, worship styles, commitments to particular schools, or our choices in pants? Is there anything that stands out?

Or, maybe better said: As you try to make your way in this world, is there anything distinctive and helpful in being part of a Reformed church?

Dear friends, for Reformed folks this morning's text is a formative story.

It's one link in a chain that runs throughout Scripture. That chain is the covenant-making activity of God. The Reformed tradition reads the Bible as the unfolding story of the covenants that God makes. We celebrate, remember, and affirm that God is a promise-making God. Our text this morning is one chapter in that promise-making story.

Consider…

Earlier in Genesis God promises Abram and Sarai – two old, dry, nomadic wanderers – that they will have land and children. But decades pass, they survive famines, they take refuge in Egypt, they amass great wealth, they wage war, they grow older, and there is still no sign of a child. God's promise stands in sharp contrast to their barrenness.

In fact, Abram is so convinced that it's all little more than wistful wishing that he takes matters into his own hands and draws up a will to pass on his possessions to a favored servant. Whatever God had promised, it didn't seem rooted in the reality that Abram knew.

So, God drags Abram outside to look up at the stars and invites him to start counting…

> This was not the handful of stars that push through the reflected light of a city sky. This was not the flickering of a few stars against the ambient light of the suburbs. This was the pitch-black darkness of the wilderness, and the sky spangled with millions of billions of stars and the clouds of faraway galaxies, quasars, and nebula. This was a cosmos that's expanding outward at an ever-increasing speed – all the while birthing new stars.

And, to one without a son, God says, "So shall your offspring be." God doubles down. "Not only will you have a child, but you will be father of more than can be numbered…"

God makes the intangible promise vivid and graphic and intergalactic. And then, dear friends, there's this lynch pin line in the covenantal chain.

> *Abram believed the Lord, and it was credited to him as righteousness.*

You have to wonder what happened. What changed?

> Was Abram impressed by the starry-starry night? Was he persuaded that if God could make all these stars, he could kindle life in an old womb? Was there something in the tone of God's voice? Was he somehow convinced and convicted by the case God made? All we're left with is Abram mute and looking up at the night sky.

Walter Brueggemann gets at it this way:

> *What moved Abraham to a new response? Surely it was not because he feels new generative powers in his loins. Nor because he has new expectations for Sarah. The new promise for his life is not any expectation of flesh and blood. Rather, he has come to rely on the promise speaker. He has now permitted God to be not a hypothesis about the future, but the voice around which his life is organized.... The new pilgrimage of Abraham is not grounded in the old flesh of Sarah nor the tired bones of Abraham, but in the disclosing word of God.*

Beautifully put; may we have such faith. May our lives be so organized around the promises of God. But…

But you'd think all of that – the stars, the voice of God, the belief – would be enough to stir up a resolute confidence in Abram. And yet again he pushes back with doubts and questions, "Look, Lord, about the land… How can I be sure…"

Abram, who was credited with righteousness, still wrestles, wonders, and questions God about the promises. He's still looking for more proof. He's still looking for something on which he can hang his hopes.

This is followed by an enigmatic recounting of God engaging Abram in some sort of ancient-oath-taking-ritual with blood and smoke and critters cut in half. The Hebrew word for covenant derives from the root "to cut," hence the messy business of dividing animals in half and both parties passing between them to confirm the covenant. But, like Adam sleeping when Eve is created from a spare rib, Abram is sound asleep through the culmination of the ritual…

Some read here a foreshadowing of God bearing the curse even as we break covenant. But I don't want to get hung up on that part. I want to get back to the old guy in the shower and what's distinctive about the Reformed tradition.

Anne Lamott was a writer, alcoholic, single mom, and self-described wreck – with a nagging sense that despite how hard she ran, God was tracking her down. She thought of God as an alley cat who wouldn't leave her alone. Listen to this description:

I thought it was just an apparition, born of fear and self-loathing and booze and loss of blood. But then everywhere I went, I had the feeling that a little cat was following me, wanting me to reach down and pick it up, wanting me to open the door and let it in. But I knew what would happen: you let a cat in one time, give it a little milk, and then it stays forever. So I tried to keep one step ahead of it, slamming my houseboat door when I entered or left.

Later, when life was ruptured and chaotic, she walked out of a church service…

I began to cry and left before the benediction, and I raced home and felt the little cat running at my heels, and I walked down the dock past dozens of potted flowers, under a sky as blue as one of God's own dreams, and I opened the door to my houseboat, and I stood there a minute, and then I hung my head and said 'F— it: I quit.' I took a long deep breath and said out loud, 'All right. You can come in.' So this was my beautiful moment of conversion.

God pursues us. From that first moment when God goes looking for Adam and Eve, to picking out Abram and making promises, to entering into creation in Christ, to steadily padding after each of us like an alley cat, God pursues us.

Abram doesn't go looking for God. There is no indication that Abram was a seeker who forged a relationship with God because of his discipline and dogged determination. Rather, the story reads that when Abram was 75 God came to him.

The initiative was God's.
The pursuit was God's.
The promise was God's.
Thanks be to God.

All throughout scripture God pursues us and makes promises with us. What he wants in response is relationship. He wants to be the voice around which life is organized. And Abram's response gets credited as "righteousness" by God. Belief squares things up with God. All that God counts here is trust – trust that God will keep his promise.

Seems simple enough. And yet, throughout the rest of scripture, the people on the other end of the covenant fail to live up to their end of the deal. Over and over again they fall away and forget,

slip up and screw up,
deny and doubt,
waffle and walk away.
They behave just like me and you.
And still, relentlessly and repeatedly, even unto death, God pursues them to renew the covenant.

Dear friends, Reformed folks emphasize God's covenant-making activity. We rehearse and remember, not our faithfulness, but the faithfulness of God. The theological gift or emphasis that we share is the good news that without precondition, God seeks after us – promising to be our God and we, his people.

As it turns out, we're the shining stars of God's promise to Abram.

You're a shining star – belonging to God, through the promises of God.
You're a shining star – created and redeemed by God in Christ.

May our lives be ordered in response to those promises. May we come to the table as a sign and seal that those promises are fully realized in Jesus Christ. And in turn, may we share with others – for the promises are not ours but belong to as many stars as are in the sky.

Amen.

Where All Ladders Start

GENESIS 28:10–19

William Butler Yeats, early twentieth century poet, wrote late in his life about a loss of imagination and inspiration. The poem, "The Circus Animals' Desertion" laments a diminished sense of wonder and muse and ends with these lines:

A mound of refuse or the sweepings of a street,
Old kettles, old bottles, and a broken can,
Old iron, old bones, old rags, that raving slut
who keeps the till. Now that my ladder's gone,
I must lie down where all the ladders start
in the foul rag and bone shop of the heart.

Listen to that last line again:

I must lie down where all the ladders start
in the foul rag and bone shop of the heart.

In Ireland, when Yeats wrote, a rag and bone man would push a handcart around the city to gather up refuse in the hopes that some of it could be resold for any purpose, even as compost. A rag and bone shop was a resale shop.

Yeats writes that he's left with life's debris. Ravaged and scavenged, all he has is decaying, vulnerable, mortal stuff. He's down to the frailty and failings of the human heart. Everything else is stripped away. There's nothing left but the place where all ladders start.

It's a poignant and powerful picture.
It's a picture of where we find Jacob.

Consider…
Jacob swindled and suckered his brother. He conspired with his mother to trick his father – who has now sent him away to take a bride. He's a scoundrel on the run. He's transient, stripped of all pretense, power, place or piety, at night in the middle of nowhere, alone, vulnerable, between a rock and a hard place, amid foul rags and bones, and he lays down to sleep…

And God breaks in.
God props up a ladder to heaven.
God comes to Jacob in a dream.

For thirteen years we had a handsome golden retriever named Phil. He was broad shouldered, gentle hearted, lazy, and well loved. He slept on the floor by our bed. Every once in a while, in the middle of the night, he would let out a long mournful howl – a wail that broke your heart, scared small children, and woke the neighbors. It was haunting and mysterious. I'd roll over, with my heart racing, to check what was wrong, only to find him sound asleep. He was dreaming.

I hope he dreamed of being a young puppy bounding across a grassy knoll after something stinky. I wonder what he dreamed that gave rise to a mournful howl.

A doggie therapist might suggest that in his dreaming some unconscious reality was breaking through to consciousness. Some part of his psyche, some piece of his past, some puddle of self-disclosure was trying to come to the surface. Or, maybe his doggie brain was just randomly processing the memories and meals of that day.

Of course, we've learned not to put too much stock in dreams. In the words of Walter Brueggemann,

> *We children of the Enlightenment do not regularly linger over such illusive experiences as dreams. We seek to "enlighten" what is before us and to overcome the inscrutable and eerie in order to make the world more manageable. We do well in management while we are awake, and we keep the light and power on 24/7. Except, of course, that we must sleep. We require sessions of rest and thus of vulnerability. Dreams address us. They invite us beyond our management.*

God addresses Jacob when he is not in control.

Unbidden, unmanaged, God intrudes. He doesn't track down Jacob as a seeker in a sanctuary or one of the faithful at an altar; he doesn't come at Jacob's behest. Rather, God interrupts when Jacob is not looking. He finds Jacob in a mundane moment of human vulnerability. God comes to Jacob where Jacob is…

And, maybe that's a good place to begin.

One remarkable claim of the Old and New Testaments is not that God creates and gives commandments, but that God intervenes. God invades. God breaks into history, into human life, even into our lives.

> And that's a staggering claim. For while it suggests that we're not alone in "this thing called life," it also leaves open all sorts of possibilities of how and when and to whom God might come.

We build temples, mosques, and churches to engage God.
We practice rituals, liturgies, and sacraments to encounter God.
We long after God in art, music, and poetry.
We search for God…

And yet God turns up where we least expect him: in a dream, to a barren old couple, in a manger, on a cross, in the rag and bone shop of the heart.

Where has God intruded in your life?
Where has God dropped a ladder?
When you weren't in control, when you least expected it, when you were asleep, where did God break in?

In this first dream in scripture, Jacob sees a ladder.

That "ladder" was probably more like a ramp. Mesopotamian ziggurats were huge layered land mass temples, often times with steps leading to the next level. They were believed to connect heaven and earth and be the dwelling place of the gods. Chances are the tower of Babel was one of these ziggurats; and chances are that Jacob's dream was of something similar.

Jacob sees angels scurrying up and down this "stairway to heaven," and God is either at the top of the ladder or somehow beside Jacob. When Jacob wakes, he says that God was "in" this place. Either way, the dream suggests that the membrane between heaven and earth is permeable.

There's an intertwined, overlapping, unified creation.

There's no secular reality and a separate sacred reality.
Jacob is not pulled up into some otherworldly spirituality.
God doesn't sweep him up out of his mess.
God comes to Jacob in a particular place in time and space and affirms the promises that he made to his father, grandfather, and grandmother.
God breaks in and says:

> *I am the Lord, the God of your father Abraham and the God of Isaac. I will give you and your descendants the land on which you are lying. Your descendants will be like the dust of the earth, and you will spread out to the west and to the east, to the north and to the south. All peoples on earth will be blessed through you and your offspring. I am with you and will watch over you wherever you go, and I will bring you back to this land. I will not leave you until I have done what I have promised you.*

Now. I know that this reaffirmation of God's covenant is the big deal in this text. I know that this is one more chapter in the unfolding drama of salvation history. God is making promises that run from Jacob, through Jesus, to beautiful little Ari Rose in her baptism this morning. Thanks be to God.

But I'm still stuck with the humanity of Jacob and the ambush of God. Does God show up in self-authenticating ways when we're in dire straits, in desperate need, and down to our last card? Is the dream of Jacob a window into the nature of God?

Many of us can offer testimony that some existential-reality-of-God showed up in a therapist's office, at an AA meeting, on the side of a bed in the oncology unit, or on the mourner's bench. And I know that many of us are longing for the same.

For, the truth of the matter is, I don't know one of us who isn't broken. I don't know one of us who doesn't have issues. I don't know one of us – who if you strip away our accomplishments and our middle-American safeties and sensibilities – isn't left with foul rags and bones.

Religious practice can be a cover. Class and culture and the illusion of control will carry you only so far. But at some point, life will lay us bare.

At some point, I'll be uncovered as an imposter.

But, as the gospel is true, then it is precisely when we're laid bare that God breaks in. When we're empty handed, when we're lost, when we're scared, when we're dead, that's where God finds us. That's where all ladders start.

John Buchanan puts it this way:

> *That is the basic thrust of biblical faith: "I am with you … in the world. The world is my focus." God comes to us in our humanness: where we are most human, which means in our frailties and weaknesses, in our doubts, in our anxieties and fears, in our hopes and dreams. God comes to us in our disappointments, our failure to be good and strong and honest as we want to be. God comes to us in our guilt, our betrayals and deceits, as God came to Jacob.*

I'm sure there are other ways that God breaks in, but if God would come to a "died-in-the-wool, double-barreled con artist" (Frederick Buechner) like Jacob, then surely God would come to me, or you, or to some other. For who are we to limit how far and wide God's mercy extends?

Dear friends, the good news is that God dropped a ladder to Jacob. The good news is that God took up residence in these rags and bones in Jesus, whose last words in the Gospel of Matthew are:

> *I am with you always, to the very end of the age.*

Thanks be to God.
Amen.

Singing with the Symphony

PSALM 19

I went hiking with two juvenile delinquents.

One was kind of a weasel; the other was good-hearted but made bad choices. Both trafficked in mischief and mayhem, but I enjoyed their company, and there was something hopeful and lovable in both – even the sneaky one.

There are 46 mountains in the Adirondacks that measure over 4,000 feet. Climbing all 46 is an upstate New York tradition. We were going to conquer one. In the morning we hiked over hill and dale through birch and pine, my friends chattering and scurrying around like chipmunks – joking, sneaking cigarettes, and trying to bait me with dirty jokes. In the early afternoon the pitch got steeper as we scrambled over big boulders and up one substantial escarpment.

Once we were out of the woods the pace quickened – as if some urgency was pulling us to the top. Above the tree line the wind had bite, the sky was a furious blue and gray, and at the summit, for as far as we could see, was a mountain-topped horizon. Everything felt wild and free and unplugged,

unclogged,
unfiltered,
offline…

Then we did what seems to happen every time I've climbed a mountain.

> Without being told to do so, we drifted apart to our own spaces. We stood or sat on rocks. We didn't talk. Without prompting, for 20 minutes we listened to the symphony of creation. For a few moments this little company of ne'er-do-wells, over 4,000 feet up, soaked in the overwhelming goodness of creation – and maybe the overwhelming glory of God.

Dear friends, the psalmist's deep trust is that creation bears witness to God. The skies will sing, the mountains will rumble deep unto deep, the rivers will bubble and blabber along in joyful harmony, and all creation will join in a language that doesn't need translation. John Calvin, in the preface to a French translation of the New Testament, puts it this way:

> *The little birds that sing, sing of God; the beasts clamor for him; the elements dread him, the mountains echo him, the fountains and flowing waters cast their glances at him, and the grass and flowers laugh before him. Truly there is no need for long searching...*

And in that, Calvin and the psalmist are onto something. There is no need for "long searching," for all around us creation sings unto God. Creation is not a commodity to be consumed but a symphony that sings of the glory of God.

Barbara Brown Taylor in *Leaving Church: A Memoir of Faith* tells it this way:

> *I know plenty of people who find God most reliably in books, in buildings, and even in other people. I have*

found God in all of these places too, but the most reliable meeting place for me has always been the creation. I have always known where to go when my own flame was guttering. To lie with my back flat on the fragrant ground is to receive a transfusion of that same power that makes the green blade rise. To remember that I am dirt and to dirt I shall return is to be given my life back again. Where people see acreage, timber and soil, and river frontage, I see God's body.... The Creator does not live apart from creation.... When I take a breath, God's Holy Spirit enters me.

Maybe you've heard creation singing the mighty power of God. Maybe your flame was kindled by timber, soil, and running river. Maybe you've heard that voice with no speech, with no words, with no sound. Thanks be to God.

Ah! But it's the second part of Psalm 19 where things get dicey. For, the psalmist abruptly shifts from singing about creation to waxing poetic about the *Torah* – which is the law, or instruction, of God.

All good deists and delinquents love the first part of Psalm 19: God is an amorphous-anonymous-transcendent-deity who creates for all a beautiful, complex, and verdant world. And yet, while creation may belt out glory like a Broadway tune, the Creator doesn't have a face. God's works are on display in the heavens, but his name is as elusive as trying to count the stars in the night sky. God reveals himself in creation but in a general, generic way.

Early on in *The Institutes of the Christian Religion* John Calvin writes:

> *It appears that if men were taught only by nature, they would hold nothing certain or solid or clear cut, but would be so tied to confused principles as to worship an unknown god.... It is therefore in vain that so many burning lamps shine for us in the workmanship of the universe to show forth the glory of its Author. Although they bathe us wholly in their radiance, yet they can of themselves in no way lead us into the right path.*

Gulp! Calvin suggests that the glory of God in nature is not enough. I am not sure that the psalmist is trying to make the same point, but the psalm does take a dramatic turn after verse six.

Psalm 19 offers two frames for the glory of God: Creation and *Torah*.

In the same way in which creation declares the glory of God, so too does the *Torah*. In the same way in which creation bears witness to God, so too does the Law. In the same way that creation can open up in your soul a sense of awe or fear, so too would the *Torah*.

The dicey part (for a deist) is that this second frame is specific.

The *Torah* is a God with a name.
The *Torah* is God with a people and a story.
The *Torah* is God with a will for humanity.
The *Torah* is God with a religious tradition.
The *Torah* is God as specific.

Maybe the point of the psalm is that you need both.

As the sun illumines the *Torah*,
so the *Torah* illumines the sun.
As creation reflects the face of God,
so the *Torah* reflects the face of God.
There is one song; there are two singers.
There is one God; there are two frames.
You need both.

And again, Calvin is helpful here. He writes that we're like "old or blurry-eyed men" with "weak vision," who can barely read "two words" without glasses. Therefore, we need the "spectacles" of scripture to clear up the confusion and show us God. We need both. In order to make out the glory of God we need creation and scripture. Neither is wholly sufficient…

Pity the one who thinks he will find God with only creation.
Pity the one who thinks he will find God with only the Bible.

Allow me a little aside here…
I think this premise is important. It strikes me that we don't come to know God without nature, reason, experience, history, and all manner of things that make us human. The *Torah* doesn't drop from the sky devoid of finger prints, cultural conditions/limitations, and historical realities.

And therefore, we need all of those tools in order to understand and interpret scripture. We need the gifts of creation in order to know the gifts of scripture. Neither is sufficient unto itself.

And therefore, biblical interpretation is always in flux as we learn more from creation and as we learn more from scripture. That whole process is living, breathing – God breathed. It's not fixed or static. The church has always

> changed and moved in response to creation, scripture, and Spirit. May the same be true of us: through scripture and creation may we listen to how God calls us to love and serve both God and neighbor.

Back to our psalm…
For the psalmist this clarity of vision culminates in an expression of confession and longing.

> *Forgive my hidden faults…*
> *Keep me from willful sin…*
> *May these words and this mediation be*
> *pleasing in your sight…*

And with that turn, Psalm 19 travels from the heights of heaven to a hidden corner of the human heart. From a high peak of the Adirondacks, we've come to the interior of our own souls. We've gone from singing with the symphony of creation to whispering before God.

Dear friends, I'd offer that a biblical spirituality includes the movement of Psalm 19.

> A full-orbed human spirituality would mean time in creation, time in scripture, and time in confession. There may be other practices that lend themselves to health and faithfulness, but attention to the created order, listening to scripture, and time in solitude before God seem essential.

Therefore, let us be those who join the symphony of creation in declaring the glory of God. Let us sing with those courageous first buds of spring. Let us tend after creation as if our children's lives depend on us. And let us take our children with us into both the expanse of the wild and the mysteries of mitochondria – trusting that there they will encounter some hint of God.

But let us also be those who join in the holy racket of scripture that sings of a creating and redeeming God. Let us put on the spectacles of scripture that we might see rightly. Let us listen and learn with humility and with the expectation that God is still speaking through scripture and Spirit.

Finally, before God, and without fear, let us tell the truth of who we are. Let us learn to rest, meditate, and breathe – in doing so may we know God's forgiveness and God's pleasure. And in that may we find strength and peace for the journey.

Amen.

The Whole Alphabet

PSALM 25

The woman who cuts my hair is searching for a spirituality that's pragmatic, authentic, and a receptacle big enough for life's loves and losses.

A lapsed Catholic, she enjoys the energy of an evangelical mega-church, tries new age healing practices, and has been down an alcohol-soaked path of marriage, divorce, dating, and returning to live with her husband. She wants friends, realistic answers, and things to go her way; but she's exhausted by the search, simultaneously bored and overwhelmed by the spiritual smorgasbord of modern American life. She prays that this next AA retreat will give her what she's looking for…

I think she's like a lot of us – searching for a spirituality that can hold life's joys and sorrows, that resonates with our experience, and that's accessible.

Spirituality seems essential to being human.

Every class, creed, and culture know some expression of spirituality. Except for the most strident materialist or ardent atheist, the vast majority of people believe in a spiritual reality beyond this physical reality. There's something more than just atoms, genes, and evolutionary patterns.

> And human history points to a deep longing for an experience of that other reality. The story of our collective religious impulses is a long-universal story. My barber is not alone in her desire for connection to the spiritual, to a Higher Power, a god, a love…

Dear friends, the Psalms are a songbook of human spirituality. They're songs of praise and lament, blues and ballads, regal anthems of joy and desperate lonely cries. They're songs of protest and melodies of love. They give expression to the whole range of human experience and emotion, and they bear witness to an engagement with God.

But we – my barber, for example – often want something more exciting, more engaging, and more mindful of the complexities and general cussedness of the contemporary world. Reading, singing, or sitting with the Psalms requires a discipline, a patience, and an openness to a certain aesthetic.

Martin Luther counters with this line:

> *The Psalter is the book of all saints; and everyone, in whatever situation he may be, finds in that situation psalms and words that fit his case, that suit him as if they were put there just for his sake, so that he could not put it better himself, or find or wish for anything better.*

Clearly a child of his sexist times, Luther sees the Psalms as a record or mouthpiece of human spirituality. They offer a robust spirituality for the fullness of human experience. And that's quite a claim. Which brings us to Psalm 25…

Psalm 25 is an acrostic.

The first letter of the first word of each verse follows the order of the Hebrew alphabet. For a largely limited or illiterate people, it served as a memorization tool. It helped get this song on people's lips and in their hearts. And it was also meant to suggest the fullness of life:

from A to Z,
from alpha to omega,
from aleph to tau,
from beginning to end…

This psalm is meant not for a little segment of life, the spiritual part, but for the whole part – for the whole alphabet of life. And therefore, the psalmist offers his or her whole self. The opening line "In you, Lord, my God, I put my trust," is probably better translated, "To you, Lord, I lift up my soul…"

What's lost in translation is our arms outstretched, lifting up. Think of the birth of Simba in *The Lion King*. The psalm images us lifting up the fullness of our lives, our identities, our hopes and fears, our very selves to God.

Psalm 25 is not an invitation to self-help. It doesn't cut corners like the student who only wants to know what will be on the test. It's not written by one who thinks he or she knows better, or is looking for a technique for success. Rather, the first move, the beginning place of the psalmist's spirituality is surrender. It's offering up our lives…

As I've encountered young people with alcohol or addiction issues, I've known pretty quickly when I'm in over my head. So, I've tried to hook them up with therapists or addiction counselors. I've also taken a few to their first AA or NA meetings.

> For a couple kids, it worked; for others, not so much. What sticks out is knowing that they weren't ready when they'd report that they weren't as bad as those people, or that they thought they'd do recovery on their own.
>
> Those that stayed gave up power. They admitted they were powerless and decided to trust the program. They turned to recovering addicts, they got sponsors, and they said, "I'll do whatever you tell me to do…"

Psalm 25 has that spirit. In offering up the fullness of our lives to God, we set aside our tendency to think we know better. The psalmist asks, without precondition,

> *Show me your ways, Lord, teach me your paths. Guide me in your truth and teach me, for you are my God and Savior, and my hope is in you all day long.*

Cultivating a full-orbed-biblical-spirituality begins with offering up our hearts to God and then asking to be taught.

Thomas Boogaart writes this:

> *The human heart is permeable and heavily influenced by the various powers in our world, although we tend to think the heart is autonomous and its own master. The heart is more like a cloud shape-shifting in the air currents than a rock washed up on the lakeshore. The heart is open to the influence of the Spirit who comes and dwells there, but is also open to the influence of other spirits, for example, other people ranging from parents, to teachers, to pastors, to the proverbial "Joneses" with whom we want to keep up. The heart is also open to the*

> *influence of the culture around us—culture's values and rituals have heart-shaping power...*

And that's to say that developing this spirituality is a long, slow, process. All sorts of forces are shaping our permeable and porous hearts. And the humility required to open our hearts to God's instruction can just feel like too much...

Others do the same and end up at differing places of interpretation or practice, so why bother? Why try? Why put in the effort? Why keep trying?

We get comfortable,
we get set in our ways,
we get bored,
we get overwhelmed,
we get jaded,
we get cynical,
we get busy,
we get...

Again, I think Psalm 25 is instructive.
Listen again to this line:

> *Show me your ways, Lord, teach me your paths. Guide me in your truth and teach me, for you are God my Savior, and my hope is in you all day long. Remember, Lord, your great mercy and love, for they are from of old.*

The psalmist offers up his or her heart to be taught, because of God's *great mercy and love*. In Hebrew those two words are *raham* and *hesed*.

Raham (compassion or mercy) is linked to the Hebrew word for "womb." God's mercy is tied closely to the concept

> of "womb love," the love a mother feels for her yet-to-be-born child. It's a mercy that comes from the womb of God.
>
> *Hesed* is God's covenantal love. It gets translated as unfailing love, loyal love, lovingkindness, faithful love. A love that never fails, never runs out, or walks away.

Dear friends, the reason the psalmist pursues this spirituality is the *raham* and *hesed* of God. The requests – take me and teach me – are only possible because of God's great mercy and unfailing love.

A few years ago, Hope's very own Gary Meyer wrote a piece for the Calvin College alumni magazine in which he told the story of how a rough-cut farm boy from South Dakota found his way to be a student and a teacher. He told how his big hands, made for pushing a plow, ended up pushing a pen. The story turns on Gary getting a freshman term paper back from a professor with this note:

> *I am giving you a D– on this paper, Gary, only because I am so disgusted with what passes for college caliber these days, and I am fighting it almost single-handed, but don't kid yourself – this is nothing but an F paper. Rewrite!*

Gary goes on to recount how he learned to write at Calvin but more importantly how he was also given a vision for what it meant to live as a Christian. Then Gary ruminates on the Calvin College symbol – a picture of a heart being held out in a hand surrounded by these words, "My heart I offer to you, Lord, promptly and sincerely." Gary ends his essay with these lines:

> *Here is my question about the motto: Whose hand is holding the heart? I always thought that it was my hand offering my heart. Now I am beginning to see that it may be better seen as my heart in God's hand.*

That's a wonderful nuanced distinction. Out of longing and trust we offer our hearts to God, only to discover that God has been holding us all along – with great mercy and unfailing love.

> *Show me your ways, Lord, teach me your paths. Guide me in your truth and teach me, for you are my God and Savior, and my hope is in you all day long.*

The whole alphabet of Psalm 25 offers the beginning place for a robust human spirituality. Therefore,

whoever we are,
wherever we are,
whatever we're facing,
may we know the depth and breadth of that mercy and love,
and may our spirituality be rooted in the same.

Amen.

Industries of Fear

ISAIAH 43:1-7

Dear Friends…

> *This is preeminently the time to speak the truth, the whole truth, frankly and boldly. Nor need we shrink from honestly facing conditions in our country today. This great nation will endure as it has endured, will revive and will prosper. So, first of all, let me assert my firm belief that the only thing we have to fear is fear itself – nameless, unreasoned, unjustified, terror which paralyzes needed efforts to convert retreat into advance.*

With those words, Franklin Delano Roosevelt inaugurated his presidency in 1933. The United States was wedged between two world wars and mired in a deep trough of the Depression. National confidence was at low ebb, solutions were elusive, and recovery seemed like a mirage. The moment was precarious. The President-elect needed to chart a course for the country. And he began by talking about fear.

The rest of the speech had a solemn, religious quality. For example:

> *These dark days will be worth all they cost us if they teach*

us that our true destiny is not to be ministered unto but to minister to ourselves and to our fellow men.

FDR called for commitment, sacrifice, and seeking the common good, but he began with fear.

The only thing we have to fear is fear itself.

Maybe FDR was on to something.

There was reason to be afraid, but people were paralyzed by fear and FDR knew that they needed to be encouraged and reassured. He knew that while fear can animate human activity, the resolution of fear is essential to human flourishing.

Before coming to Hope, if I'd been asked what themes would run through my preaching, I would have said something about Jesus, the brokenness of this world, the restoration of *shalom*, and a grace that extends beyond imagination and theological system. I don't think I would have said anything about fear. I didn't know what FDR knew.

But after almost 20 years, I'm struck by how often fear is a central thread in scripture. I don't willy-nilly pick passages for preaching; they're prescribed by the lectionary, but over and over again I've lifted up a thread about fear.

Consider our text…

The people of Israel were battered by years of war, were the victims of ethnic cleansing, and were abandoned in a foreign land. Jerusalem was in ruins and the Israelites were singing songs of exile in Babylon. As strangers in a strange land, with the boot of the oppressor on their throats, they were mired in a deep trough of powerlessness. National confidence was at low ebb, solutions were elusive, and recovery seemed like a mirage. They were paralyzed with fear…

The text we read from Isaiah corresponds with that historical reality; it's from a section often called the Book of Consolation.

> *But now, this is what the Lord says – he who created you, O Jacob, he who formed you, O Israel: "Fear not, for I have redeemed you; I have summoned you by name; you are mine…. Do not be afraid, for I am with you…"*

Over and over, with every turn of the page, with every turn of events, God's response to the human experience:

> *Do not be afraid, for I am with you.*

Thomas Long writes:

> *If you had to put the Gospel of Jesus Christ into one phrase, I think it might be, "Do not be afraid." It is what the angels said to the shepherds in Bethlehem when Jesus was born: "Do not be afraid." It is the first word the angel spoke on Easter morning: "Do not be afraid." It is what the risen Christ said to his disciples: "Do not be afraid. I am with you always."*

At birth, death, and resurrection: Do not be afraid.

Rick Warren counts 365 variations of that command in scripture. That count seems a little too tidy…

But no matter how deep the water or how high the flame,
no matter how hard the road or how heavy the load,
no matter how long the journey or how dire the straights,

God says,

Do not be afraid, for I am with you.

However, what about when there's good reason to be afraid?

Sunday school teacher and former President Jimmy Carter released an essay recently with this line:

> *I now fear that what we have fought so hard to achieve globally — the right to free, fair elections, unhindered by strongman politicians who seek nothing more than to grow their own power — has become dangerously fragile at home.*

If you pay attention to a particular strain of news, you'll fear that democracy is under siege and civil war is coming. If you swim in a different news-media-eco-system, you'll fear the loss of individual freedoms, hordes of lawless immigrants, critical race theory, Antifa, entitled welfare recipients, and jihadi terrorists…

We fear either the virus or the vaccines, the Proud Boys or Black Lives Matter. We fear socialism or insurrection, the corruption of voting integrity or the loss of voting rights. We fear censorship or unfettered lies. You get the idea…

I'm not arguing a moral equivalence between these two competing visions. I'm not suggesting equal footing regarding objective truth. But, no matter how or where we consume news, we participate in industries of fear. They stimulate and stoke our fears. They promote and profit from fear. We live in an age where anxiety has been commodified. We live in a culture of fear.

Of course, some fear is clearly situational. If you're being chased by a pit bull or you've eaten spoiled meat there's reason to anticipate discomfort and rightly be afraid. But human development theorists point toward fear as more than just a function of culture or situation. Fear is fundamental in the shaping of human personhood.

This will feel like Psychology 101…

Abraham Maslow suggested that we have a hierarchy of needs, and as the lower needs are filled, the higher needs emerge. At the base of our pyramid is the need for food, water, air, sleep; but the very next fundamental need is a sense of safety, security, and belonging. We can't move and grow unless there is resolution to fear.

Erik Erikson believes that we all pass through developmental stages, and each stage is characterized by a different "crisis" which must be resolved so that we can move on to the next stage. If we resolve a particular stage in a broken or incomplete manner, we will struggle and revisit that "crisis" later in life. Erikson's first stage and his last stage are fundamentally about trust and fear. A healthy baby won't fear life; a healthy adult won't fear death. And almost every stage in between has some vestige of the dynamic of trust and fear.

You get the point. We all fear. Fear is an essential part of being human. The issue, the question, the crux of it seems to be how we respond to fear, or how we live with fear.

> And I don't mean the resolution of fear through safer neighborhoods, healthier diets, or a more robust democracy. I mean the resolution of fear, or how we live with fear, as central to who we are. And that gets at our faith or our sense of God…

Dear friends, if one thread in scripture is fear, the other thread is belonging.

> Over and over in scripture, at every turn of the page, at every turn of events, God seeks after a people to be his own. One can't lift up the thread of fear without finding it woven with the thread of identity and belonging.

Therefore, these few lines from Isaiah locate Israel's response to fear in both creation and redemption. And I think it's worth noting that Isaiah is writing here to a people and not to the interior lives of individuals. This is meant for a collective, for a community, and Claus Westermann notes that at this point the Israelites were

> *a tiny, miserable, and insignificant band of uprooted men and women standing on the margins of a hostile empire...*

But to them the Lord says, I created and redeemed you. Therefore, don't fear, for you are mine. The One who made you and saved you will never leave or forsake you. Ultimately, therefore, there is nothing to fear.

God doesn't promise that we'll be protected from those things that rightly scare us. We'll still be overwhelmed by the waters, singed by the fire, and struggle on the journey. Being created and redeemed by God doesn't spare us from dying of cancer, getting hit by a car, or struggling with depression.

> But the word of God through Isaiah is that we don't face those realities alone. We belong to a God who will never abandon us. So, while perfect love might cast out all fear, the resolution of fear is primarily a function of identity.

> *What is your only comfort in life and in death?*
> *That I am not my own, but belong, body and soul...*
>
> —Heidelberg Catechism

At birth, death, and resurrection, you belong to God.
At birth, death, and resurrection, don't be afraid.

Scott Hoezee puts it this way,

> *We live in the shadow of all the dear folks who died in our various congregations this past year as well as in the shadow of all those who left our congregations in a huff over mask mandates or vaccines or some other pandemic-related and deeply politicized thing. And there will be more hurt in our congregations this year. There will be disappointment.*
>
> *What we cling to in utter hope, however, is that God goes with us in and through all that. We will not be finally swept away or drowned or burned up. There will always be a new thing yet to come in God's grace and in his slow kingdom coming.*

Thanks be to God.
Amen.

Dry Bones and Dead Ends

EZEKIEL 37:1–14

Let me tell you a story.

It's a hard, coarse story.
It's a horror story.
It's a story not to be told in the company of children.
It's a story full of dead ends.
It's a story that's still being written.
Let me tell you a story.

On November 6, 1991, a band of the Charles Taylor Rebels attacked a small village in Liberia. In desert-dusty-pick-up trucks and battered Jeeps they roared into the village without warning and unleashed waves of terror. They were part of a violent uprising to overthrow the government of Samuel Doe.

The first house they stormed was the home of Sabby Browne. Her father worked for the government as Deputy Chief of Immigration. They bound, beat, and tortured him in unspeakable ways – before they killed him. Sabby was restrained and forced to watch.

The rebels then tore Sabby's infant son Onesimus from her hands, brutally raped her, and left her to die.

Left for dead, with little food and less hope, Sabby and Onesimus crawled into the scrub brush wilderness and then walked through the "bush" (Sabby's word for the Liberian countryside) for more than a month.

> On December 10, they arrived in the Ivory Coast. A family took them in, but after three months – when they could no longer provide the care that Sabby needed – they asked her to leave. Homeless, penniless, helpless, hopeless, a young mother and her baby, at a dead end.

On March 12, 1992, Sabby and Onesimus arrived in a refugee camp in Ghana. It was crowded with tens of thousands of refugees fleeing the same horror. Sabby found work weaving hair and found a relationship with a man from Ghana. She had two more children, Rufina and Ndu. After a season the man left her – a homeless mother with three children in a refugee camp. Another dead end.

A refugee resettlement program – that knits together aid-agencies, church efforts, and the cooperation of governments – brought Sabby to the United States. A little church on a corner in southwest Chicagoland (Hope) cobbled together the money and means to welcome them to a furnished apartment. And on a bitter, bone-chilling February night in 2006, 15 years after the Charles Taylor Rebels roared into her village, Sabby and her three children arrived in Chicago.

The children were small – stunted from malnourishment.
They needed shots and medical attention.
They needed safe, strong, consistent schools.
They needed a stable community.
They needed hope.

Sabby said, “I don’t know where my mother, brother, and sisters are since the Liberian War, but I thank God that I am alive with my children.”

Two years later, after being moved around by the apartment management company, Sabby and her children found themselves in a basement apartment in a block-long building, half of which was vacant and boarded up. The electricity was sporadic, the pipes broke and flooded the apartment, cockroaches and mice were plentiful, and with no locks on the entryway, homeless men sought refuge in the hallway. Another dead end.

Again, that little church (Hope) used money from the Deacon’s Special Fund to relocate Sabby and her family to a good, clean, safe apartment. Today, Sabby works two jobs, the kids go to school, and they’re part of a community of resettled refugees. Thanks be to God.

Dear friends, you can hear in that story evidence of the remarkable resilience of the human spirit. It contains the tension between the worst impulses in humanity and the best. You can hear it as a celebration of luck, or providence, or the mystery of how some survive in this cruel world. But I invite you to hear it as a living parable of dead ends.

We run stuck in this world.
We hit brick walls.
We get mired in intractable conflicts.
We exhaust options.
We deplete hope and drain help.
We’re left for dead.
Our common denominator is dead ends.

Our stories may not be as dramatic as Sabby's, but we all have stories.

We know the dead ends of bankruptcy, cancer, depression, sexual abuse, lonely loveless relationships, unemployment, heart disease, grieving the loss of a loved one, and family conflicts that won't budge. We know the dead ends of seeking peace in Palestine or political unity in the United States. We know violence on our streets and the profound imbalance of a global economy. Dry bones and dead ends are the way of the world.

But this ancient text opens up a window, offers a vision, and gives voice to a faith.

Ezekiel's vision of the valley of dry bones is not really a story about the resurrection of the dead. Rather, it's used as a metaphor for the renewal of the people of Israel.

They were at a dead end. Exiles in Babylonian captivity, their land was ravaged, their temple destroyed, and their families scattered. Refugees in a strange land, they regarded this political and military defeat as an irrevocable historical judgment. Marduk, the God of the Babylonians, had prevailed. Yahweh had proven impotent, their faith had proven inadequate, and the covenant promises had proven insufficient. The formation of a kingdom with a king didn't turn out so well either. They went the way of all empires – they rise and fall.

Stuck in Babylon, some sat by the river and sang old songs while others scoffed. They were like a field of bones: dry, dusty, sun bleached, and dead still.

Without breath.

Without help.

Without hope.
A dead end.

Then God called Ezekiel to go stand in the middle of the cemetery. Climb up on a tombstone – with neck bones and thigh bones and wish bones as far as you can see – and proclaim:

> *Dry bones, hear the word of the Lord! I will make breath enter you, and you will come to life. I will attach tendons to you and make flesh come upon you and cover you with skin; I will put breath in you, and you will come to life. Then you will know that I am the Lord.*

Dear friends, over and over again in scripture's unfolding-story-of-salvation, this is the central hope…

Don't be fooled by dead ends.
Don't trust your eyes or ears.
Don't believe the way of the world.
Don't bet on pretty ponies, powerful kings, or piles of money.
Don't believe it when the fat lady sings.
It's not over.
Hope in God.

For when you're without power, when you're weak, when you've run out of options, when you're dead, there is still the breath of God.

And brittle bones will band together and be blown full of life,
and a dry old man and a barren old woman
    will give birth to a son,
and water will come from a rock,
and a virgin will bear a son,
and the garden tomb will be empty,
and the dead will be resurrected.

Now, that vision gets twisted into a cheap faith in long shots, and we get sold a bill of goods that if we believe enough, God will turn our scars into stars. And it skirts the role that Ezekiel's vision played in the story of God's people – for they did return home to rebuild the temple, and Babylon, that eternal empire, fell in fifty years, but…

But, be that as it may, there is still the hope that God continues to breathe new life into dead ends and dry bones. There is still the deep longing that God is at work in creation – even today. So, despite what can feel like overwhelming evidence, we cling to the hope that the breath of God will blow
  and rattle old bones,
  and marriages that are dead in the water
    will find new winds of love,
  and stone-cold drunks will get sober,
  and those embalmed with greed
    will be alive with compassion,
  and the poor of spirit and the poor of pocketbook
    will be filled,
  and those dry with depression will be drenched with deep joy,
  and this old world will be turned upside down,
  and refugees will dance of justice and mercy and peace,
  and death won't have the last word.

Dear friends, the long trenches of life remind us that the breath of God will blow where it will. Our task is to be faithful in the waiting, give thanks when we feel it on our faces, and follow its leading even when it blows toward the cross. For our confidence is not in
  our genetic pool,
  or our good fortune,
  or our earnest efforts.

> Our confidence is that God will do a radical new thing.
> Our confidence is in resurrection to restore *shalom.*

For, although we don't know the dead ends we will face in this world, we know the covenant promises of God that are realized in resurrection. And foretold by the prophet Joel,

> *I will pour out my spirit on all flesh; your sons and your daughters shall prophesy, your old men shall dream dreams and your young men shall see visions. Even on the male and female slaves, in those days, I will pour out my spirit.*

I don't know what's dead in your heart.
I don't know where death has a grip in your life.
I don't know how dry and brittle you are.
But the will of God is that life will come out of death.
Our faith is not a naïve optimism or confidence in the power of the human spirit.
Our faith is in the breath of God – breathing new life even in dead ends.

Just ask Sabby Browne.
Amen.

Locusts and the Locus of Hope

JOEL 2:12–13

In 1915, clouds of locusts stripped bare the hills and fields of Palestine.

Grains, fruits, vegetables, and all manner of vegetation were devoured by swarms of "gregarious" locusts. The resulting devastation spiked six-fold the cost of basic food stuffs and caused widespread hunger and social dislocation. *The New York Times* reported, "Sugar and petroleum are unprocurable and money has ceased to circulate."

In response, rabbis called for days of prayer, farmers used crude flame throwers to drive back these winged invaders, and politicians appointed commissions and launched campaigns. Laws were enacted requiring that all men between the ages of 15 and 60 collect 20 kilograms of locust eggs or pay a hefty fine. It was a determined human response to a plague of biblical proportions.

According to *National Geographic*, locust swarms have been measured at 460 square miles and can pack between 40 to 80 million locusts in less than half of a square mile. So…

imagine the sky black with locusts,
imagine the air thick with locusts,
imagine locusts in your hair, in your eyes, in your mouth.

Each day, each locust can eat its weight in plants; therefore, a swarm can eat hundreds of millions of pounds of plants in a day. So…

imagine every tree stripped clean of leaves,
imagine fertile fields gnawed to wastelands,
imagine locusts crawling over one another to get to that last nibble of green.

Dear friends, nothing announces the advent of Jesus like a good plague story.
Nothing says "Merry Christmas" like "gregarious" locusts.
No?
Why, then, this introduction about locusts?

There's no consensus about when the prophet Joel wrote his book, but it opens with a locust attack. Listen to these first lines:

> *What the cutting locust left the swarming locust has eaten; what the swarming locust left the hopping locust has eaten, what the hopping locust left the destroying locust has eaten. Wake up, you drunkards, and weep! Wail, all you drinkers of wine; wail because the new wine has been snatched from your lips. A nation has invaded my land, a mighty army without number, it has the teeth of lions, the fangs of a lioness. It has laid waste to my vines and ruined my fig trees. It has stripped off their bark and thrown it away, leaving the branches white…*

You get the idea. The rest of the book details other destructions, calls for lament and repentance, and offers images of a coming universal hope. But it all starts with the locusts.

Some biblical scholars read these ravaging locusts as a metaphor for an invading enemy. These are not just rampaging grasshoppers but a poetic picture of a pagan army laying siege to Israel. Other scholars read the book not as an insect infestation but as a metaphor for that which strips us clean of every pretense or prop…

Addiction can lay bare the human soul.

Cancer can shred the last vestige of human strength.

Depression can destroy the roots of hope.

Injustice can devastate the fruits of kindness.

Loneliness can level life.

Again, you get the idea.

The locusts are a metaphor for that which makes life nasty, brutish, and short.

Either way, whether Joel is writing about actual insects or using a metaphor, I think the bigger question is…

Does God employ clouds of locusts as a teaching tool?

Does God exercise judgment by raining down destruction?

Does God use plagues to teach his people a lesson?

Are natural calamities divinely directed to make a point?

Would the God who sent plagues on Egypt to wrench free his people send plagues on his people to wrench free their devotion?

What if we think about it this way?

We began this sermon series in Genesis 2, and I suggested scripture casts a conflict between chaos and *shalom*. To quote myself:

> *One way to read scripture is as a tug of war between the goodness of God's created order and the chaos of sin.*

> *The rest of scripture can be understood as a pitched battle between shalom and rebellion. A tug of war between life and death, gift and curse, light and dark, love and fear. That struggle is the dramatic conflict that animates scripture's story.*

Therefore, it seems to me that we're on shaky ground when we link natural phenomena – locusts, cancer, depression, hurricanes – to God's will.

> Rather, they seem part of the curse and chaos that cripples creation. They're part of the seething struggle that grips creation. And while it is entirely plausible that Joel interpreted a locust invasion as something to drive God's people back to God in repentance and dependence, I don't know that means God sent the locusts…

But we've also been reading that God keeps calling, commanding, chiding, and chasing after people. God pursues people to be vehicles of *shalom* for the rest of creation. God wades into this world he created and aligns himself with Abraham, Sarah, David, Jonah, Jeremiah, Joel, and a whole host of men and women that his will might be worked out.

Through promises and prophets, through kings and kingdoms, through the frail and the fallen, God pursues *shalom*. God is not static, stoic, or removed but God is active, emotional, and invested in *shalom*. And to that end he longs for our devotion and obedience to his way and will.

I did a funeral for a three-month-old baby. There was no warning or long illness. It was a SIDS death. Two wonderful, gentle, loving parents were devastated – laid bare. A grief beyond any ability to shoulder.

> I didn't know the parents very well. I sat with them, wept with them, tried to help their family and friends gather to grieve with them. I find myself worrying, praying, thinking, and longing for them…
>
> It would be understandable to abandon God in this. It's easy to feel that God abandoned them. The struggle between chaos and *shalom* is cheap talk when your heart is shattered. And it would be an abomination to suggest that God would will such a loss that they might find their way back to God. That's the behavior of a monster, not a God.

And yet, Joel writes in the darkest hour, even when the very earth shakes, even at the most dreadful, even now,

> *…return to me with all your heart, with fasting and weeping and mourning. Rend your heart and not your garments. Return to the Lord your God.*

Dear friends, in the face of locusts, whether plague or metaphor, the call of scripture is to turn and open our hearts to God. The call is to turn toward the same God who enters into creation in pursuit of its *shalom*. The call is to turn toward the same God who desires devotion and obedience.

But why?
Given every reason to abandon God, why turn toward God?

Almost lost in our translation is a wonderful little Hebrew word that shows up 240 times in the Old Testament. That word, *hesed*, is difficult to translate. It's not contained by an English equivalent. Therefore, *hesed* gets translated as loving-kindness, compassion, steadfast love, mercy, faithful love, loyal love, great love. When translated into Latin it's often *misericordia*, which is mercy plus heart.

Hesed is a loyal love. It's stronger than any disappointment.
Hesed is a covenantal love. It stretches beyond feelings.
Hesed goes beyond the rule of law. It's not based in obligation but generosity.
Hesed is love offered steadfastly, without failure or waver.
Hesed is a strong love that doesn't grow weary, faint, or fail.
Hesed is what God does.
Hesed is who God is.

Joel says return to God because he is *hesed*.

> *...return to me with all your heart, with fasting and weeping and mourning. Rend your heart and not your garments. Return to the Lord your God, for he is gracious and compassionate (hesed), slow to anger and abounding in love, and he relents from sending calamity.*

Dear friends, we turn to God because of *hesed*.

The locus of our hope is not the strength of our faith, the confidence in our insight, or even the honesty of our repentance. The locus of our hope is the *hesed* of God. In the midst of despair, laid low by grief, overwhelmed by clouds of locusts, and stripped bare, we turn toward God because his compassion is more powerful than his wrath, his mercy bests his judgment, and his loyal love is stronger than our fear.

The writer of Lamentations puts it this way:

> *Because of the Lord's great love (hesed) we are not consumed, for his compassions never fail. They are new every morning; great is your faithfulness.*

I don't know what locusts you're facing this morning. I know that for some of you they are overwhelming, the sky is dark, and the struggle is real.

But the good news is that God is *hesed.*

God has not abandoned us.

God will not abandon us.

Because of *hesed* there's mercy enough for each day – new every morning.

That would seem a good place to end. In the face of life's locusts, the locus of our hope is the *hesed* of God…

But in this season of Advent, it also seems fitting to remember that the *hesed* of God is a person. The loyal love of God is embodied in Jesus Christ – *hesed* in the flesh. The mercy-heart of God seeks after us, and becomes one of us, even unto death.

I can't say God sent the locusts any more than I can say God willed the death of a baby. But somehow, someway, beyond anything we can imagine, despite what we may feel, God was still there when the locusts attacked – he never left.

Great is the faithfulness of God.

The *hesed*, the steadfast love of God, endures forever.

Don't be afraid.

Amen.

Out of Broken Glass

MICAH 5:1–5

On a silent night, holy night,
all was calm and all was bright,
and the little town of Bethlehem lay in a deep and dreamless sleep,
when hundreds of tanks and armored vehicles laid siege to the city.

Bethlehem, in the Palestinian West Bank, is enclosed by an apartheid-like wall with a few gated checkpoints. On April 2, 2002, from five different directions, the Israeli Army invaded the city through those gates. The rationale was a suicide bombing that took place in Jerusalem a few days earlier, but the military build-up around Bethlehem had begun weeks earlier.

Bethlehem was besieged before first light. Tanks rumbled through the streets, Apache helicopters hovered overhead, and the *tac…tac…tac, tac* of machine guns filled the night sky. The army moved methodically – block by block, street by street, door by door. There was scattered resistance.

But a small band of armed Palestinian militants fleeing from the Israeli troops broke into the compound around the Church of the Nativity to take refuge or to prepare to fight. Almost sixty priests, monks, and nuns who live in the church compound were trapped inside along with other Palestinian civilians. All told there were approximately two hundred people in the church compound.

The army positioned tanks in Manger Square, set up snipers on roof tops, and used the Palestinian Peace Center as their logistical headquarters. What unfolded was a tense, bloody, thirty-nine-day stand-off.

This little town became the focus of the world's attention.
The hopes and fears of all the years, gave way to fear.
The weapons of war split the skies where the angels sang.
The birthplace of the Prince of Peace became a
  killing ground.
As the sons of Abraham killed one another in Bethlehem.

Bethlehem is an insignificant village, set in some scrub brush hills, about six miles southwest of Jerusalem. But Bethlehem's significance in the Old Testament is substantial. The stories of Rachel, Ruth, Boaz, and David all run through Bethlehem. And in our text, the prophet Micah references Bethlehem.

Biblical scholars believe that Micah was written about eight hundred years before the birth of Jesus. Written during a time of instability and imminent invasion, it's a short book that's long on prophetic rage about injustice to the poor, oppression by the rich, indifference of the rulers, and empty religious ritualism.

But right in the middle of the gloom and doom of an impending destruction there's a whiff of hope. Micah announces that out of ragtag-Bethlehem there will come a ruler whose reach will be to the ends of the earth, and from the line of David there will come a king whose reign will be peace.

Dear friends, those few lines have been picked up as prophetic foreshadowing of the birth of Jesus. Matthew writes that when Herod gathered together the chief priests and teachers of the law to ask where their Messiah was to be born, they quoted this little text in Micah. The Christ will come from Bethlehem.

And, in God's economy, there's a coming great reversal.
The poor will be rich,
the last will be first,
the servant will be king,
and the tables will be turned.

This text is another reminder that the ways of God are not the ways of humanity. From where you least expect will come what you least expect. From the last and the least, from cradle and cross, from virgin womb and sealed tomb will come what you least expect. It's a tender and beautiful text in that regard.

But there is a second, more substantial theme…
Our translation reads:

And he will be our peace

The orthodox interpretation is that this coming Messiah will not just embody peace, or inject peace, or broker peace, or teach peace, or pray for peace, but that the Christ will be our peace. Underneath that reading is the assumption that we're estranged and at war – not just with one another – but with God.

Now. That sense of humanity's relationship with God is easily dismissed.
It's archaic.
It's unenlightened.

It's rooted and gnarled with life-choking guilt.

Surely, we're at least neutral before God, or we hold a spark of God, or we're chums with God, or we're part of God. Mostly God is a mystery, but we're not at war with God. We're good people doing our best to lead good lives...

But a historically Reformed (biblical) understanding is that we're alienated from God and from one another. The foul fruit of that alienation is our broken relationships and our troubled souls. The evidence is the tanks of armies and the guns of terrorists.

Listen to the way it is framed in the Belgic Confession:

> *We believe that by the disobedience of Adam original sin has been spread through the whole human race. It is a corruption of all nature – an inherited depravity which even infects small infants in their mother's womb, and the root which produces in man every sort of sin. It is therefore so vile and enormous in God's sight that it is enough to condemn the human race, and it is not abolished or wholly uprooted even by baptism, seeing that sin constantly boils forth as though from a contaminated spring.*

Gulp!

That harsh assessment of humanity is hard to swallow.

And yet, if in fact we're alienated from God, the good news of Micah is that

in a time of occupation,
in this little backwater village,
in the crude comforts of a stable,
in a humble fashion – unbidden and unexpected,

> to a young mother and a bewildered father,
> God slipped into the pool of humanity to be our peace.

The gift of Christmas is that God in Christ is our peace and there is therefore – nothing to fear. We're reconciled to God. The war is over. Death is defeated. And the peace of God which transcends all understanding holds our hearts and minds. Thanks be to God!

Merry Christmas!

Today, Bethlehem is poor and predominately Muslim. When I was there, we passed through layers of security and under armed turrets to get into the village to get to the site where Jesus was born. Which, incidentally, is tensely and clumsily shared or managed by the Armenian Church, the Roman Catholic Church, and the Greek Orthodox Church. Each with its own entrance to the tiny cave where the tiny babe was born...

While there, I sat in silence in the upper sanctuary and tried to listen for God. I'd had my fill of caves, religious clutter, and churches as museums. It all seemed so time trapped, distant, disconnected, and dead. Maybe it was just me...

> But then we went to the International Center of Bethlehem – a Lutheran school, college, arts program, economic development project, worshipping church, and health and wellness community center. And there, I saw the church vibrant and alive.

During the siege of Bethlehem, the Israeli Army positioned tanks in the Center and destroyed in eleven hours what had taken seven years to build. But out of that rubble, this church,

Christmas Lutheran Church, and the International Center were rebuilding their life and ministry.

A bright young Palestinian woman gave us a tour. She couldn't talk without a smile and an easy laugh. And, in the heart of a place where children know the names of missiles by the sounds that they make, and where workers wait three or four hours every day to go through the gates to get to their jobs, and where you can't buy or bring back books...

She said, that after forty days of siege, when families hid in their homes, and no one worked or walked the streets, and schools were destroyed, and water and food were in short supply...

After forty days of waiting and worrying and wondering about the boot that was pressing down on their throats...

After forty days of siege when the children came back to the International Center, Pastor Mitri Rahib said that rather than pick up rocks to throw at the tanks, and rather than pick up guns to kill in revenge, they would pick up broken glass...

So, they went about the city and picked up the shards of shattered windows. And then their artisans began to make stained glass angel ornaments out of the broken glass. And today they have a thriving web-based gift shop that ships these tiny symbols of peace all over the world.

In Pastor Rahib's words:

We choose to respond to the culture of violence with the power of culture... shaping new symbols for a new reality, transforming the symbols of destruction and war into symbols of hope and peace.

Angel ornaments out of broken glass in response to Apache helicopters.

Dear friends, may it be so with us. Because Christ is our peace, may we take the broken glass of our lives – whatever gifts and shattered shards we hold – and use them for the *shalom* of others. May our lives be marked not by revenge and greed but by forgiveness and mercy. May peace not be relegated to our souls but may it be that which prompts us to pursue reconciliation with friend and family, with neighbor and enemy.

May we be artisans of broken glass because…
on a silent night, holy night,
 when all was calm and all was bright,
 and the little town of Bethlehem lay in a deep and
  dreamless sleep,
 God slipped in as a baby, and the angels burst out in song:

Glory to God in the highest and on earth peace…

May the peace of Christ be with you.
Amen.

How it Happened

LUKE 2:1–20

Maybe it's all those crèches on front lawns and coffee tables.
Maybe it's due to illustrated children's Bibles.
Maybe it's because I never thought it might be any different…

But I always pictured Mary and Joseph arriving at an inn late at night – the sky inky-black, the stars twinkly, and the only light a flickering oil lamp. In my imagination the inn is a square adobe structure with a couple windows and a thatched roof.

Joseph sheepishly knocks on the wood door as Mary winces while easing herself down off the donkey. The innkeeper comes to the door in a robe with his tousled-hair stuffed up into a night cap. He wants to help, but he looks over his shoulder and with a shake of his head and a shrug confirms that he just doesn't have any spare rooms.

You get the idea.
Maybe you thought the same.

Joseph looks down at his dusty sandals. His shoulders slump. There's a chill in the air. And he's just about to muster up the courage to plead, when the innkeeper brightens with an idea.

"You could go out back to the stable. You could build a little fire. The hay is dry and you could sleep on that. It'd be better than trying to travel more – given her condition."

And, Jesus is born in a barn of warm-worn-woods, soft lights, and gently lowing cows. At least that's the way I pictured it, given all of those crèches in front yards and on coffee tables…

However, while in Israel I saw that everything was stone – white-sunbaked-broken-hard-scramble-stone. Big boulders and chipped pebbles. Rock-faced cliffs and stone caves. There's tillable soil, but mostly, most everything was rock.

And while in Bethlehem, a Palestinian woman told us that chances are Mary and Joseph showed up at a cave with a structure toward the front where the family ate, slept, and lived, but toward the back of the cave there was a place where the animals were kept – with stone mangers and stone troughs.

Bethlehem is in the occupied West Bank hills, where there's a sort of geological-logic to Jesus being born in a stone cave. And quite frankly, the word translated as "inn" can be better translated as "lodging place." Meaning the place where the people slept.

And given that the front of the cave was probably already full of folks who were in town for the census, Joseph and Mary were probably offered the space in the back where the animals were kept at night…

And Jesus was probably born in a cave-dwelling built into the side of a West Bank hill with animals being sheltered from night predators.

I guess how it happened doesn't really make a big difference, but it serves as a reminder that God in Christ is born in a particular place, at a particular time, with the particular idiosyncrasies that make things particular.

As my friend Father Torey Lightcap writes:

> *It is, in one sense, a very great scandal that God should choose a little boy – a baby – in some cave somewhere in which to be seen. In a time and in a place to which we can point on a map or a calendar. It's as outrageous as it is sublime. The stink and spittle of animals, the blood of birth, dirt floors, uncertainty, terrible humility.*

It's as outrageous as it is sublime.

There's a mystery here beyond imagination and fairy tale. God born as Jesus with the DNA of Mary. God born as Jesus with the DNA of the Holy Spirit. The very breath of divinity coughed out of the lungs of a newborn with a tiny-little-bottom-wrapped-in-cloth, in the back of a cave. God as flesh on stone.

Tradition places the Church of the Nativity atop the site where Jesus was born. Down a skinny-set-of-stairs, in a cramped basement grotto, you stoop down to see a 14-pointed silver star set into a marble floor surrounded by silver lamps where, according to tradition, Jesus was born. Then you're nudged forward to another altar marking the site where Mary laid the newborn baby in the manger. The Orthodox Church manages the birth altar; the Catholic Church manages the manger altar…

For almost two thousand years Christians have come to this site believing in and looking for evidence of the Divine. When

I was there it was standing room only as Asians and Ethiopians, Eastern Europeans and Southern Baptists, Brits and Hispanics, Catholics and Pentecostals were all wedged together in the basement hallway, with cameras in hand, hoping to get some sense, some feeling, some hint that God had been there.

And that, dear friends, is part of the wonder of Christmas.

> We're gathered not because of idea, creed, or confession. We are gathered not just for music and family traditions – no matter how beautiful. We're gathered together because in a particular place, at a particular time, God became mass and matter. We're gathered in the faith that God took on cells and cellulose. We're gathered in the mystery that God slipped-in among us.

There is a specific context and specific cast of characters: The bean-counters conducting a census to expand the tax-rolls for Caesar Augustus, the calloused hands of a confused carpenter, the swollen ankles and sore back of a pregnant woman – traveling ninety miles by donkey, a stone-feeding-trough as a makeshift cradle, gasping for breath in labor, and a mother peering over her belly for a glimpse of the baby. God umbilically tied to a poor Hebrew girl.

Henry Langknecht gets at it this way:

> *Mary didn't give birth to an avatar or a name or an idea. Mary didn't give birth to a host of representative samples of humanity's diversity. Mary gave birth to one human baby whose annoying specificity warns us and protects us, first from worshiping only our favorite icons, and second from worshiping only the cosmic Christ, the eternal Logos or any other philosophical tag in whose inscrutability we*

can claim Christmas unity. Jesus already and only looks like Jesus.

The incarnation is a scandal because of its specificity.

God became this and not that.

God took male shape and not female shape.

God as a Hebrew and not a Native American.

God as poor, vulnerable, and tossed aside – not middle class, powerful, safe.

The "annoying specificity" of a God who is not just universal-cosmic-Christ but also God with fingerprints is scandalous. And yet, in the words of Wes Granberg Michaelson:

The God who brought billons of galaxies into being chose to enter into earthly human life as a vulnerable baby. If this is true then every human life is given a point of contact with the Creator. Then the God who brought everything into being is not some remote and distant force far removed from our daily lives. Rather, then this is a God who does the miraculous in order to be with us; and every human life can be impregnated with the divine presence.

Every human life is given a point of contact with the Creator.

I like that. Not only is there the specificity of God in Christ but there is the specificity of God and you.

When the angel announces the birth to the shepherds, the angel says:

> *Do not be afraid. I bring you good news of great joy that will be for all the people. Today in the town of David a Savior has been born to you…*

In Greek the personal pronoun "you" here is plural. It has the sense of "all y'all." But this plural personal pronoun is also in the dative case.

Nothing screams "Merry Christmas" like a little grammar lesson, but…

> English doesn't have a dative case but Greek does. The dative case is reserved for things that come directly to another party. The dative would be used when I give a gift to you, or I pull you aside to say something directly to you. The dative is personal in the sense that something is being directed quite specifically your way. The emphasis or exclamation of the dative case is that the action is specific, to you.

Therefore, the announcement of the angel is not a generic all-purpose bulletin. The announcement is personalized. This good news is for you. Listen to the announcement again:

> *Do not be afraid. I bring you good news of great joy that will be for all the people. Today in the town of David a Savior has been born to you; he is the Messiah. This will be a sign to you…*

Bring you…
Born to you…
Sign to you…

The scandal is not just the "annoying specificity" of God but the "annoying specificity" of you. This good news of great joy is for you.

God for you.
God with you.
God beside you.
God in you.
Each of you.
All of you.

Martin Luther put it as a question:

> *Of what benefit would it be to me if Jesus would have been born a thousand times and it would have been sung daily in my ears that Jesus Christ was born, but that I was never to hear that Jesus Christ was born for me?*

Dear friends, between that which is outrageous and that which is sublime, may you know that God came not as a proposition but as a person, born in a stone cave and nailed to a wooden cross, for you. And in that may you know peace – real, tangible, eternal peace. In that may the world know peace – real, tangible, eternal peace.

And no matter how it happened, may that love slip – quietly and unmistakably – into your particular life even on this particular morning.

Amen.

Hometown Hero

LUKE 4:14–21

How does where you come from shape who you are?
Is your worldview determined from whence you view the world?
Does your hometown matter?

Jesus grew up in Nazareth.

Located in Galilean hill country, first century Nazareth was an insignificant Hebrew village of maybe only four to five hundred people. Much of the housing was caves or huts built into the side of a slope. There's little evidence of trade or agriculture of any consequence, and there's no mention of Nazareth in the Old Testament or the Talmud. In the Gospel of John when Nathaniel asks, "Can anything good come out of Nazareth?" he may have been besmirching more than just its size. Nazareth was the other side of the tracks. It was a dog-eared, two-bit, no-account, scrub-brush town.

But, just over the hill, about an hour walk from Nazareth, was Sepphoris.

Sepphoris was located at the intersection of two trade routes. You can see it from Nazareth. It was politically connected, culturally rich, militarily important, and beautifully cosmopolitan…

There were stone-paved roads and Roman columns.
There were bath houses and detailed mosaics.
There was a theater and a market.
There was a synagogue and an aqueduct.

A first century historian referred to Sepphoris as "the ornament of all Galilee." In fact, many scholars think that when Jesus said that "a city set on a hill cannot be hidden," he was talking about Sepphoris.

A good deal of Sepphoris was built on the backs of cheap Hebrew labor. And, while some of the architectural beauty of Sepphoris was built after Jesus, the foundation, the character, and the contrast between Nazareth and Sepphoris was built or being built during the first thirty years of Jesus' life.

So, it seems entirely plausible that if Joseph (the father of Jesus) was a carpenter or a stone mason, the only work he would have found was in Sepphoris. It's entirely plausible that most mornings Joseph and Jesus would have hiked over the rise to work at building this cosmopolitan-city-jewel.

Our text this morning reads as the coming-out-party for Jesus. He returns to his hometown synagogue on the Sabbath, and as the neighborhood kid who was making quite a splash, he was handed the scroll of Isaiah to read. How he landed on this particular passage is unclear, and what we have recorded is an odd splicing together of a couple verses and phrases from Isaiah, but Luke writes that Jesus read:

The Spirit of the Lord is on me, because he anointed me to proclaim good news to the poor. He sent me to proclaim freedom for the prisoners and recovery of sight for the blind, to set the oppressed free, to proclaim the year of the Lord's favor...

Then, as he sat down, taking the posture for preaching, people pressed in to hear his first sermon and Jesus threw down the gospel gauntlet.

Today this scripture is fulfilled in your hearing.

The word here for "fulfilled" could better be translated as "filled-full." It means to cram a net, level a hollow, or fill to the brim. It's a word that describes a completed accomplishment. There is nothing more to do, nothing more to add. The time is ripe, arrived, full. It's now.

When I was in Israel I stood on the sun-bleached-stone-streets of Sepphoris and wondered if Jesus ever felt like a kid from the other side of the tracks. Standing where the ruts of Roman wagon wheels are still visible, I wondered if Jesus thought of himself as poor. Did he know the Roman boot on his throat? Did he walk back to Nazareth with the day-laborers, listening to their laments and longings? Does where you come from determine how you see the world?

Because when Jesus stood up to read in his hometown synagogue, he didn't turn to a text about the beauty of the earth or the glory of the heavens. He didn't pick a passage pointing to repentance or scan the scroll for scripture about sin. Jesus didn't preach about belief or read a verse about doctrinal purity. Instead...

Jesus read to the poor and the marginalized
that the good news was theirs.

Jesus read to the oppressed and imprisoned
that they were free.
Jesus read to the blind that they could see.
Jesus read to a bunch of co-workers and friends that the city on the hill was a mirage, that the kingdom was at hand, and that they were no longer rejected outsiders, but were accepted, emancipated, and the day of the Lord's favor had arrived.

It was a stunning short sermon with an audacious application. It shook his neighbors to the core. They didn't know what to make of it. In a few short verses they'll run him out of town, he'll go from hometown hero to hometown heretic, but initially they're amazed and maybe even caught up in the vision.

Dear friends, historically-theologically-practically the church has softened the edges of Jesus' reading of Isaiah. We've done Jesus the favor of reading his first sermon through the filter of history and the lens of privilege...

Surely Jesus meant all of this spiritually. Jesus didn't mean that the doors of the jail should be unlocked – he was speaking metaphorically. Or, Jesus wasn't suggesting that Nazarene day-laborers would get a fair wage. And surely, he didn't mean that the blind would really see.

The good news was for the poor of spirit.
Freedom was from the captivity of sin.
The recovery of sight was spiritual vision.
Sin is what oppresses; therefore, liberation was
from damnation.

Right?

When I stood in the ruins of Sepphoris and looked toward Nazareth, spiritualizing this text barely made sense. If what I saw of Nazareth and Sepphoris was true, then what Jesus proclaimed must have also been real, tangible, earthy, and physical. It seems like a cruel joke if Jesus says to the poor and oppressed that their mansion is in heaven and he's simply going on ahead to prepare rooms for them.

> It seems more likely that the Hebrews saw the mansion on the hill, and this announcement by Jesus from Isaiah was about the coming of a tangible, earthy, physical justice, freedom, and *shalom*. And not simply a spiritual reality...

I want to be clear. I'm not dismissing a spiritual interpretation, but I'm wondering if there's something more. Can our reading of this gospel story be filled-full?

Today, when Sepphoris is an architectural ruins and Nazareth is a bustling city, how should we read this text? How do those separated by time, place, and position understand this proclamation?

Let's come at it this way...

In 1863, President Abraham Lincoln issued the Emancipation Proclamation. The South had seceded, the union of states was in tatters, and the Civil War was taking an enormous toll. The proclamation declared "that all persons held as slaves" within the rebellious states "are, and henceforward shall be free." Lincoln, in his claim to authority over the whole of the split union, contended that the proclamation was true and real. He proclaimed that the slaves were free.

However, the slaves who lived within the Confederacy remained in bondage. Many didn't even know about the proclamation.

Its authority was denied and nullified by local and regional powers. And yet, in reality, from Lincoln's perspective, they were free. As the union was restored, as confederate states assumed their rightful place, and as the slaves came to realize their freedom, their emancipation was already a reality.

My apologies to history teachers and Civil War buffs, I know that the proclamation didn't include the north and some border states. I know that real freedom was realized more slowly and with more complexity – not unlike our freedom. But the image seems helpful…

For Luke, this announcement in the synagogue is the inaugural address of Jesus.

> The Kingdom had arrived. The time was full to the brim. Their emancipation was already a reality. They just didn't know it yet. And then in the next few chapters, Luke stacks up snapshots of the lame being made to walk, the blind being made to see, those in chains being released, and the dead being raised. He offers evidence of this new reality.

Jesus read a hope that was etched deep in the souls of those Hebrews with bent backs; he tapped into an ancient image of a coming day when God would put creation to rights. Then he said, "Today is that day…"

> He didn't offer a new vision or call for them to grab pitch forks and storm Sepphoris to remake reality. He didn't change their economic situation, but he did announce the arrival of a new reality in which they could live into the way of God.

Dear friends, may it be so with us. May we have the faith that in Jesus of Nazareth – God has come and is coming.

And therefore, may we hope, believe, and live like *shalom* is ultimate reality and that love will ultimately win.

> And because that's true we're free to seek justice, cherish mercy, and walk humbly with God. We can pursue equitable economies, we can work for freedom from whatever imprisons, we can see the imprint of God's image in all and seek their flourishing. We can love friend, neighbor, and enemy in honest, practical ways because our current relationships are not the end of the story. We can seek reconciliation, speak the truth, and traffic in forgiveness.

We're a long way from first-century Nazareth. Our hometowns have shaped us in powerful ways. We don't always recognize the ways in which we're enslaved. But as those upon whom God's Spirit is poured, we are called to live into our emancipation. We are free to follow the way of Jesus…

> *anointed to proclaim good news to the poor, freedom for the prisoners and recovery of sight for the blind, to set the oppressed free, to proclaim the year of the Lord's favor…*

Amen.

Dancing, Drinking, and Glory

JOHN 2:1–11

Our daughter's wedding was preceded by a year of planning and preparing, a year of discussions and decisions, a year of waiting and wondering and worrying and…

> And then the day arrived. Skies were blue and lightly sprinkled with puffy white clouds. Dresses, tuxes, flowers, and candles were tastefully and gracefully appointed. With Vivaldi on violins, liturgy, laughter and love danced among us in the wedding ceremony. At the reception food was abundant and drinks overflowed while the sun set over the lake in a breathtaking blaze of oranges and reds. And as Lauren and Sandi's dreams were realized I couldn't have been more grateful.

I don't know what the father of the bride is supposed to feel; I know that I had all the feelings. I was a complicated knot of love, loss, longing, gratitude, regret, joy, pride, insecurity, delight, relief, hope, and happiness. As the father and officiant, I worried that when I opened my mouth that knot of feelings would unwind as a bawling blubbering mess.

Late that night as the reception rollicked along, the bartender kept coming up to me with an update on the bar bill.

"Mr. Nelson, this was our estimate; this is where we are right now. Do you want to continue?" Gulp…

Around me people were dancing and drinking. My daughter was in the center of the dance floor, my son-in-law was at the bar surrounded by the West Michigan chapter of Young Republicans, I didn't know what the father of the bride is supposed to feel but shutting off the tap seemed in poor form. We needed a wedding reception miracle.

We needed water into wine, or gin, or…

Where's Jesus when you need him?

Dear friends, it's remarkable to me that John opens his gospel with this story. Given all the troubles in the world, why rescue a wedding reception with what seems like a magic trick? John only includes seven signs or miracles in his gospel; why lead with this one?

Let's sit with the story for a few minutes.

Jesus was at a small-town wedding in the Galilean foothills.

Jewish weddings were colorful affairs that lasted seven days. There were rites and rituals and the transfer of dowries; there was merriment and meals and joyous good will. But this reception ran out of wine, and with no party store around the corner, there would be no quick fix.

Mary drew Jesus' attention to the dilemma. He wondered why it was his problem. Where was the father of the bride? But, as only a mother can, Mary translated his hesitation as a willingness to do something, and she told the servants to follow his instructions.

Jesus spied empty stone jars that were used for ceremonial

purification. If the wedding had been going on for a few days – these were the empties. These were the jars used up by all the rules for rigorous religious cleanliness. So, Jesus sent the servants to the well. "Fill the jars with water."

Six jars, at thirty gallons a jar, that's one hundred and eighty gallons. That's a lot of water. And boom! Jesus turned that well water into fine wine. That's a lot of wine. The maitre d' confirmed the quality and pulled the bridegroom aside to voice his astonishment: "This is an unheard of extravagance! You saved the best till last! Let the dancing and drinking continue!"

We often read this story as a metaphor. Jesus is inaugurating a new covenant. The old laws and legalisms are empty; the new container overflows with grace. Edward Markquart puts it this way:

> *Jesus took 180 gallons of Jewish laws, and rituals of purification, and transformed them. Jesus took 180 gallons of guilt, 180 gallons of laws, laws and more laws, 180 gallons of don't do this and don't do that, 180 gallons of laws that numbered more than 600 regulations, and he transformed them into a new religion, a new meaning, a new wine that would bust old wine skins....180 gallons of guilt are transformed into 180 gallons of grace.*

That's a wonderful reading of this story.
The old is gone; the new has come.
  There's no judgment,
  there's no wag of the finger,
  there's no picking of nits,
  there's no guilt.
  There is extravagant forgiveness.

As John puts it,

> *Out of his fullness we have received grace in place of grace already given. For the law was given through Moses, but grace and truth came through Jesus Christ.*

Thanks be to God.

I've done a lot of weddings. I've done weddings in trailer parks, castles, cathedrals, and refurbished furniture factories. I've officiated on beaches and bluffs, in gardens and on golf courses. I've been soaked by sweat and drenched by rain. I've yelled over passing freight trains and whispered through quiet tears. I am richly blessed to have been part of so many beautiful, hopeful, joyful moments.

But I am also aware that weddings are remarkably unremarkable. Across class and culture, across race and religious inclination, for almost every people group in human history, weddings are part of life. While the rituals and rigmarole might be different, the essentials are similar: two people, surrounded by loved ones, a solemnization of the commitment, and then food, drink, and celebration. For all the investment in a special day, there is something decidedly common. Weddings are an almost universal tradition.

Which points back to our text.

There's no mention that the bride or bridegroom knew who jump-started their reception with the good wine. There's no indication that Jesus did anything to call attention to what he did. The text reads that only the servants and disciples knew. As John puts it:

> *What Jesus did here in Cana of Galilee was the*

> *first of the signs through which he revealed his glory; and his disciples put their faith in him...*

This story is more than a metaphor; this is an epiphany. And John, or Jesus, use the setting of this decidedly common-human-day to offer a glimpse of the glory of God. We typically associate glory with some sort of luminous transcendent presence, but here, rather than blazing clouds and smoke on the mountain, glory is Jesus helping keep a party going.

Scott Hoezee puts it this way:

> *Glory is big. Glory is bright. Glory is loud. Glory is a multisensory extravaganza that you will not miss if you are anywhere in glory's neighborhood when it happens. But when Jesus quietly transformed water into wine in an effort to do no more than solve a social mishap that helped a family save face in front of their friends, this was somehow Jesus' first revelation of no less than his glory. Indeed, this glorious manifestation was sufficient as to cause the disciples to put their faith into Jesus...*

God as one of us – born of a woman, from a s—hole town like Nazareth, dancing at a wedding, reluctantly obeying his mother – is the glory of God. The glory is not in shiny lights; the glory is in the incarnation. And that, dear friends, is the outlandish claim of the gospels: the fullness of God into the fullness of human life. As John puts it a few verses earlier:

> *Now the Word became flesh and took up residence among us. We saw his glory—the glory of the one and only, full of grace and truth, who came from the Father.*

And this glory is first revealed at a wedding reception…

So, while this text may be a metaphor, it's also an affirmation of the created order. It's an affirmation of human life and love. It's affirmation of food and drink and dance and sexuality and the knot of emotions that would leave the father of the bride a blubbering mess. The gospels proclaim that God enters into this world not to trash it, torch it or take us out of it, but to love, redeem, and reclaim it. And therefore, God enters into the beauty of a wedding but also into the darkness and banality of human brokenness, suffering, and death…

Irenaeus, second century church father, wrote that "the glory of God is a human being fully alive." And this text is a picture of God emptied into the fullness of being human.

And! As that is true, then hints, or glimpses, of God's glory must still be present in this world. God wouldn't create and enter in only to abandon. The affirmation of the created order points to the mystery that God is present and still speaking into this world.

Frederick Buechner puts it this way:

> *If I were called upon to state in a few words the essence of everything I was trying to say both as a novelist and as a preacher, it would be something like this: Listen to your life. See it for the fathomless mystery that it is. In the boredom and pain of it no less than in the excitement and gladness: touch, taste, smell your way to the holy and hidden heart of it because in the last analysis all moments are key moments, and life itself is grace.*

Dear friends, while this story may be a metaphor that God is doing a new thing in Jesus Christ, it is also an indication that this world, these bodies, are the arena of God's glory.

> It's ours to pay attention to. It's ours to give thanks. It's ours to love and honor every image bearer of God – from Haiti, Africa, or Norway. It's ours to marvel at the mystery that God so loved the world that he entered in. It's ours to look and listen for God's presence – even today.

Thanks be to God.
Amen.

Note: *An essay by Scott Hoezee was very helpful in both flow and content.*

First, Blessing

MATTHEW 5:1–12

Benediction by Ken Haruf is a novel set in a small town on the Colorado high plains. In an early scene the new preacher in town is stepping into the pulpit during a time of war and turns to the Sermon on the Mount. He encourages the congregation to take Jesus at his word. He says that there's no reason to spiritualize the words or think that we know better, but we should do exactly what Jesus says. And he begins to talk about love besting hate, and light overcoming darkness, and…

And then this:

> *But then he was abruptly halted. Someone out in the congregation was talking. Are you crazy? You must be insane! A man's voice. Deep throated. Angry. Loud. Coming from over on the west side of the sanctuary near the windows. What's wrong with you? Are you out of your mind? He stood up, a tall man in a light summer suit staring at Lyle. You must be crazy as hell! He turned fiercely and grabbed his wife's hand, pulling her to her feet and gesturing angrily at their little boy. They came out of the pew and went hurrying back up the aisle and through the doors and out of the church.*

Others followed suit and by the novel's end they've run the preacher out of town.

Interpreting the words of Jesus is risky business. Gloss over what he says, try to soften the edges, and you run the risk of selling your soul as a dispenser of spiritual bromides. Take him at his word and you run the risk of looking for new work.

And yet here we sit with the first lines of the Sermon on the Mount. The opening stanzas of which are beautiful, poetic, and mysterious – seemingly anchored in a dramatically different world than the world in which we live. They're like lovely embroidered wall hangings, little reminders of some other mercy but disconnected from day-to-day reality.

For in this world, blessed are those with swagger, not those poor of spirit. In this world, blessed are those who celebrate victory, not those who are broken with loss. In the world that I know, those who are strong are blessed, not those who are weak-meek-or-mild. In the world that I know, blessed are those who strive for success, not those who are starved for justice…

You get the idea. The opening of the Sermon on the Mount seems impractical, impossible, and other-worldly. As Kurt Vonnegut put it, "Vocal Christians, often with tears in their eyes, demand that the Ten Commandments be posted in public buildings. I haven't heard anybody demand that the Beatitudes be posted anywhere."

So, dear friends, what are we to make of the Beatitudes?

Do they have anything to say to those who live in the real world?

And again, let me point out the incongruity of a middle-aged man, in a middle-sized, middle-class church in middle-America, trying to make sense of the words of a first-century itinerant rabbi from the West Bank. Stuck somewhere between wanting to be faithful and wanting to keep his job.

Let's set our text in context…
Matthew writes that Jesus called his first disciples and then went throughout Galilee healing every imaginable disease and proclaiming that the Kingdom of God was at hand. Crowds begin to follow. So, Jesus went up the hills that tumble into the Sea of Galilee and sat down with his disciples. In Luke's version Jesus stands and speaks up the hill to the crowds. In Matthew's he climbs up the hill and sits down with his disciples.

Imagine the crowds scattered at the base of the mountains. Jesus sees them at a distance, and then to his first followers he says,

Look. Blessed are the poor in spirit for theirs is
the kingdom…

He's not offering a new set of commandments.
He's not making promises: if you do this, then I'll do that.
He's not exhorting or encouraging.
He may not even be speaking about the disciples.
He seems to be teaching his disciples about the nature of the kingdom.

In this kingdom the blessing of God extends
to the poor in spirit…
In this kingdom the blessing of God extends
to the grieving…

Jesus is teaching his disciples that everything they've thought about the world is backwards. In the Kingdom of God, the first shall be last, the last shall be first, and the blessing of God extends to those whom you would least expect. This is the way of the Kingdom. This is the new world order.

N.T. Wright puts it this way:

> *If we think of Jesus simply sitting there telling people how to behave properly, we will miss what was really going on. These blessings, the wonderful news that he's announcing, are not saying, "Try hard to live like this." They are saying that people who already are like that are in good shape. They should be happy and celebrate…*

Now. That seems crazy to me! Or least overstated.

Who would say to a parent grieving the death of a child, "Blessed are you who mourn… Be happy and celebrate." Or to one carrying the scars of sexual abuse, or stripped of power by the toxic march of a terminal disease, "Blessed are the poor in spirit… You're in good shape." That kind of lunacy would rightly get a preacher run out of town.

What if we come at it this way?

The word here for blessing is *makarios*. It can be translated as blessed, fortunate, well off, deeply content, happy, etc. It's a slippery word that's hard to nail down, but in this setting, it conveys God's favor.

> *Favored of God are those who are merciful for they shall be shown mercy.*

And that favor is both present and future…

> *Favored of God are those who mourn* (present tense) *for they will be comforted* (future tense)

And! The language of blessing here is performative: the pronouncement of blessing actually conveys the blessing. The language is not hortatory: "We ought to be poor in spirit…" or, "Let us be meek…" or, "We must hunger and thirst for righteousness…"

The blessing of God is not earned by what we do.
The blessing of God is an act of grace, realized in the pronouncement.
The blessing of God is true as it is spoken.

It's worth noting that the Beatitudes appear at the beginning of the Sermon on the Mount, before a single instruction is given, before there's been time for obedience or disobedience. If the blessings were only for the deserving, they would be at the end of the sermon, prefaced with the conditional clause, "If you have done all these things…" But appearing at the beginning, they say that God's favor is primary – preceding all our efforts.

First, blessing.
Everything else follows.

Therefore, Thomas Long likens the Beatitudes to the Preamble of the Constitution. He puts it this way:

> *The Beatitudes proclaim what is, in the light of the kingdom of heaven, unassailably true. They describe the purpose of every holy law that follows, the foundation of every custom, the aim of every practice of this new*

society, this colony of the kingdom, the church called and instructed by Jesus.

Dear friends, the favor of God is granted to those who are tossed aside or left behind, to those who are poor in spirit, meek, mourning, merciful, hungering for justice, pure of heart, the makers of peace, and to those mistreated for the cause of justice…

On those Jesus pronounces God's blessing.
With those Jesus casts his lot.
To them is given the Kingdom of God.
Thanks be to God.

There's a scene in Hope Church's history that sticks with me.

Ellen Lubbers has Tuberous Sclerosis Complex. She has a wonderful spirit and in many ways functions like a young child. She fell a few years ago and subsequent issues have kept her confined to a wheelchair and a little less joyful in worship, but I will never forget her fiftieth birthday.

At the end of the service, before the benediction, I was starting to say something about her when she charged the chancel and gave me a big hug. Then, as we sang *Happy Birthday*, she stood front and center, with her arms open wide and her head tilted back, basking in the love and blessing of her church family. As we sang the last note, she took a bow to great applause and you didn't know whether to laugh or cry. Everybody that I saw was doing both. You couldn't better script the beauty and blessing of that moment.

Blessed are those who are pure of heart for they
will see God.

That would have been enough. That should have been enough. But then as I raised my hands to offer the blessing of God, Ellen, still standing beside me, joined in and spoke the benediction. Again, extending the blessing of God to us,

the poor in spirit,
the grieving,
the broken,
the lonely,
the doubters,
the muddled,
the messed up…

And maybe just for a moment the Kingdom of God drew near, a new creation seeped through the cracks of this old world, and the blessing of God was extended to all of us – through Ellen.

Thanks be to God.
Amen.

Side with the Seeds

MARK 4:26-34

Wedged in between the more popular *Parable of the Sower* and *The Parable of the Mustard Seed*, is this delightful, oft-overlooked, little parable that appears only in the gospel of Mark.

In *The Parable of the Growing Seed* Jesus offers a man scattering seed as a picture of the Kingdom of God. And then whether he sleeps or toils the seed sprouts and grows. Whether he sits on the porch,

whether he pulls weeds,
whether he waits and watches,
whether he waters daily,
whether he goes to the track and bets on the ponies,
the seed sprouts and grows.

The parable celebrates the mystery and miracle of a growing seed. And verse 28 is worth noting:

All by itself the soil produces grain…

"All by itself" is actually the Greek word *automatos* from which we get "automatic" or "automatically." And it suggests an odd turn of phrase.

Automatically the seed sprouts.
Automatically the seed germinates and grows.
Automatically the seed and soil and sun and rain produce a stalk,
which produces a head,
which produces a full kernel of grain,
which when it's ripe is ready for harvest.

And all of this happens automatically while the farmer is stretched out on a hammock. The whole thing has a sort of *Jack and the Beanstalk* feel.

So, what does the parable mean?

Who is the seed-scattering gardener? Is the seed Jesus Christ? Is the scattering the preaching of the gospel? If the parable points to the power of the seed or the process of germination, how then should it be interpreted?

It certainly shouldn't invite inactivity and indifference
– should it?
The point isn't passivity – is it?
The farmer still has to till and harvest – doesn't he?
Weeds choke growth, so surely, we must tend to pulling weeds
– shouldn't we?

What does the parable mean?

Dear friends, that line of questioning suggests that the parable has a simple one-to-one analogy, and that's not necessarily the case. Parables offer a window, a space, a slanted light that strangely and surprisingly illuminates what we don't typically see. And I wouldn't trust a preacher who says, "Let me tell you what Jesus really meant here." I wouldn't trust the one who is too quick to suggest explanations that don't allow for the beauty and mystery of the parable to slowly open.

> *This is what the kingdom of God is like:*
> *A man scatters seed...*

That said, let me explain it to you...

I'm reminded that Martin Luther, the 16th century reformer, in reflecting on that time of transformation, upheaval, and change, wrote:

> *I have opposed the indulgences and all the papists, but never by force. I simply taught, preached, wrote God's Word; otherwise, I did nothing. And then while I slept, or drank Wittenberg beer with my Philip and with Amsdorf, the Word so greatly weakened the papacy that never a prince or emperor inflicted such damage upon it. I did nothing; the Word did it all.... For it is almighty and takes captive the hearts, and if the hearts are captured the evil work will fall of itself.*

The Kingdom of God is like a man who scatters seed...

That is to say that the Word – the good news of God salvaging creation in Jesus Christ – will not die in the ground. The good news that God is redeeming, restoring, and making creation right will not prove barren, will not return void, and will not be defeated. Not because of what we do or what we don't do, but because of the work, the will, and the way of God.

It's easy to get cynical, jaded, and discouraged in this world. It's easy to retreat into indifference, despair, or distraction.

It's easy to ramp up our own efforts and sense of importance.

But what if the very Kingdom of God is growing in and around us?

What if outside of, and even in spite of, us the Kingdom of God is germinating? What if whether we sleep or slumber, whether we plow or plant, the seeds will automatically sprout and grow unto harvest because the power, the hope, and the mystery is in God and not in us?

The seeds are growing, the Kingdom is coming, "and all shall be well, and all manner of thing shall be well." Thanks be to God.

I have a friend with a mission statement. While not a full-blown-Jerry-Maguire-manifesto, he has a carefully crafted line that serves as a north star for his life's work and his sense of place in this world. When he weighs career choices and where to invest life's energy, he has a matrix through which to filter those decisions.

I don't have such clarity, but there is a line in a song by Wilco – that scruffy-post-modern-endlessly-eclectic-exceptionally-gifted-Chicago-based-rock-band – that has captured my imagination. I have referenced it in sermons before, and I come back to it again and again as a guiding light.

Tires type black
Where the blacktop cracks
Weeds spark through
Dark green enough to be blue
When the mysteries we believe in
Aren't dreamed enough to be true
Some side with the leaves
Some side with the seeds

Some side with the leaves.
Some side with the seeds.

I don't want to side with the leaves.

I don't want to side with cynicism and despair. I don't want to side with all that falls like dead, dry leaves. I don't want to side with greed, complacency, triumphalism, indifference, lust, consumption, individualism…

I want to side with the seeds.

I want to side with the seeds where the prisoners are liberated, the blind recover sight, the oppressed are set free, and the dead are resurrected. I want to side with the seeds of justice. I want to side with the seeds of forgiveness. I want to side with the seeds of mercy.

I want to side with the seeds.

They may seem buried at the time. They may lay dormant in the frozen tundra. They may be forgotten and trampled underfoot, but the power is in the seed – not in the farmer.

Justo Gonzalez puts it this way:

> *The farmer in the parable can trust the seed to grow according to the promise sealed in it. He must trust the seed to grow, for there is little he can do to make it grow, and nothing he can do to turn it into any other future than what is already promised in it. In due time, the seed will grow. Because the future is in the seed and not in the farmer's doings, he can "sleep and rise day and night," trusting in the promise of the seed.*

Given all the ways that one can invest life's energy, I want to invest in the promise of the seeds. And, even if, finally, they prove impotent, even if the weeds overwhelm the garden, even if this is all just a fool's charade, I'd still rather side with the seeds of the Kingdom. I'd rather trust, hope, believe, and invest in the promise of the seed.

In her book *Prayer in the Night: For Those Who Work, Watch or Weep*, Tish Harrison Warren deals with the grief of a miscarriage, the death of her father, and the silence of God. She uses Compline – the order of evening prayer from *The Book of Common Prayer* – as a way to get at these questions and struggles. Early on she writes that "faith is more craft than feeling."

> And by that she means that while grace is the first and last word of the Christian life, there is a craft, there are some essential practices, that follow. And then she offers this:
>
> *Faith comes as a gift. And any artisan will tell you that there is something miraculous about their craft.... A gardener cannot make daffodils grow, nor can a baker force the alchemy of yeast and sugar. And yet we are given means of grace that we can practice, whether we like it or not and these carry us. Craftsman – writers, brewers, dancers, potters – show up and work, and participate in a mystery. They take up a craft, again and again, on bad days and good, waiting for a flash of mercy, a gift of grace.*

Dear friends, I think the call of the Christian life is to take up our craft – day after day. I think it's to side with the seeds through prayer and congregational life, participating in the sacraments, seeking the *shalom* of creation, loving neighbor and enemy – these are means of grace. Even as the power is in the seed and not the weed, ours is a craft of gratitude.

I am sure there's ample reason to wring our hands at the decline of the church, the erosion of common civil bonds, the toxic cesspool in which we swim, and the gross inequities of this world. And I know that there is enough horror to buckle the knees and break the heart, but there is also this good news:

> *This is what the kingdom of God is like:*
> *A man scatters seed...*

Thanks be to God.
Amen.

Laughing at Jesus

MARK 5:21–43

Jairus did what any father would do.

When his daughter was a toddler, he loved that moment after her bath when she would be all wrapped up in a towel and crawl up in his lap for a story. She smelled like Eden before the fall.

When she played soccer with the boys, she was all laughter, limbs, and determination. As she scraped and scrambled, he stood on the sidelines with the other parents soaking in the God-given joy of the moment.

When she learned to play the flute, it was all squeaks and whistles without any sense of time. She wanted to forget it and play outside; he kept trying to get her to practice. Until finally he'd give in and let her go. The sun would catch her hair as she ran through the door, her eyes flashing with mischief as she would call out, "I love you, Dad." It took his breath away. Every time.

And when she fell asleep, he would come in and kiss her gently on the head, so as not to wake her. From the deepest places in his heart, he would whisper thanks to God.

Jairus did what any father would do.

He worked hard to provide the best garden in which she could grow. He climbed the ladder at the synagogue. He knew some call from God, and he wanted to serve faithfully and use his gifts for good, but religious work was also the best way that he knew to make a living,

to provide a home in a safe neighborhood,
to afford the best schools,
to ensure a healthy diet,
to have a place for his family to flourish.

Jairus did what any father would do.

When his daughter started to lose energy and her eyes dimmed, he took her to the doctor – right away. He asked all the questions he could think of, but he still lay awake at night worrying about what they'd missed and wondering what more he could do. Twelve-year-old girls were supposed to be bundles of boundless energy, not pallid and knocked down by pain.

So, he carried her to every doctor in the region, and he tried alternative healing practices. He would move heaven and earth, spend his last dime, and if he could, trade places with her in a heartbeat. But she kept slipping further and further away. He felt lost, impotent, desperate, and from the deepest place in his heart he pleaded, bargained, and banged at God's door.

Then word spread through the village that Jesus of Nazareth had returned from the west side of the Sea of Galilee. Jesus was an itinerant rabbi; the buzz was that he was powerful in word and deed – even healing the sick. So, Jairus did what any father would do. He ran to find Jesus.

When Jairus crested the hill just outside of town he could see a crowd gathered by the shore. He wanted to gather his dignity and catch his breath, but in love and longing he stumbled down the slope. He pushed, pulled, panted, and people parted until he was standing before Jesus – eye to eye, man to man, breath to breath.

The weight of all of it buckled his knees, and he fell at the feet of Jesus. A stunned hush rippled through the crowd. Powerful and proud synagogue leaders deferred to no one, but all professional trappings disappeared and from the dust a father begged Jesus:

> *My little daughter is dying. Please come and put your hands on her so that she will be healed and live.*

Jairus did what any father would do.

It's the beginning of a story that resonates deeply with us.

It's the interruption to the story that's harder to understand.

As the crowd jostles toward the house of Jairus, a woman – who suffered with a hemorrhage for twelve years – sneaks up behind Jesus and touches his cloak. She was a desperate woman. She'd done everything she could – tried every doctor and spent every dime – but her condition kept getting worse, not better.

In a culture where religious laws defined community, she was an outsider.

Her condition pushed her to the fringes. She couldn't participate in the monthly purification rites required of all Jewish women. She couldn't marry, couldn't join others in work or worship, and couldn't live in the community.

She was marginalized, ostracized, isolated, alienated, and cast out.

Rosemary Reuther writes of her:

Jewish law regarded a woman with a flow of blood as unclean and polluting anyone else she touched. Jesus' reaction to the woman shows his deliberate discarding of the taboo, while the woman's own terror at being discovered in touching his garment reveals her awareness at violating the taboo.

Maybe she was more like Jairus than first glance suggests; from both ends of the social strata, two desperate and courageous people crossed over social boundaries in the hope that Jesus could heal.

However, they also offer remarkable distinctions:
Jairus is prominent; the woman is of no account.
Jairus rushes forward; the woman sneaks up from behind.
Jairus is looking for a miracle;
the woman is looking for magic.
Jairus is advocating for his daughter;
the woman is on her own.
Jairus is an insider; the woman is an outsider.
Jairus has a name; the woman is anonymous.

They offer remarkable distinctions, and the longing for healing is no respecter of persons, but Jesus meets them by crossing over boundaries, breaking the rules, and touching the untouchable as he heals the woman and revives the daughter. Thanks be to God.

But…

But what hooked this preacher, this time, is the crowd laughing at Jesus when they arrived at the home of Jairus. Jesus is too late. The little girl is too dead. She is traveling down the tunnel toward the light. Her heart has stalled and her blood is running cold. So when Jesus announces that the girl is not dead but asleep, they laugh…

There's something cruel here. In the home of a heartbroken and desperate father, in the presence of a woman Jesus called "daughter" as he freed her from her long suffering, people still had the nerve to laugh. They laughed at Jesus.

Maybe it's easy to laugh at Jesus. He's so naïve, so pie in the sky, so storybook soft, so misty and gauzy around the edges.

In the real world people die.
In the real world children get sick and don't wake up.
In the real world women end up lonely and alone.
In the real world call a doctor, call an undertaker, call in the professionals.
In the real world those who upset the social order get crucified.

Maybe the laughter was mocking derision. At best Jesus was just one more spiritual-nut-bar that offered a misguided kingdom for fools, and at worst he was a religious charlatan preying on the hopes and fears of the desperate. Maybe to them it was all a charade.

Or maybe the laughter was the cynical cackle of pseudo-intellectual hipsters. They simply dismissed and disdained belief because they were sure they were smarter. Rational skepticism always sees one more question and always poses one more problem. They couldn't believe or wouldn't believe because they couldn't shake the questions…

> Religion is a product of culture, so who's to say whose religion is right? Why revive that little girl, what of the countless other fathers with dead daughters? What quirky coincidences conspired to create this situation? Simpletons and the silly cling to ancient tales of miracles – every culture has similar fables. Why is this any different?

And so, they laughed.
Jesus was a fool.
They knew better.

Dear friends, Barbara Brown Taylor writes:

> *Every healing, every revival, every banishment of evil is like a hole poked in the opaque fabric of time and space. The kingdom breaks through and for a moment or two we see how things will be – or how they really are right now in the mind of God – and then it is over. The disciples go back to their rowing, the once blind beggar walks off to look for work, the little girl stretches her arms above her head and takes the bread her stunned mother holds out to her.*

What if we read the story of Jairus and his daughter, and the story of the bleeding woman, as punctures in the veil wherein we get a glimpse of the in-breaking kingdom of God?

Our text is part of a series of stories that Mark stacks up where Jesus exercises power over the physical world, over the spiritual world, and here, even over death.

We get here an already glimpse of the not yet. We get a glimpse where the purpose of God in Christ is made clear. For God in Christ would cross every boundary so that sin – and every twisted expression of sin – will be defeated and death will have no final hold. And dads won't bury daughters, and women won't be tossed out alone. And this story is an invading and inviting picture of what is in Jesus and what will be in Jesus. It is a picture of a kingdom come and a kingdom coming.

And as that is true, then
no matter how dead you feel,
no matter what death you're dying,
no matter where you're bleeding,
the good news is that the very nature of reality is changed.
In Christ the Kingdom has broken in.

Is that too much to hope,
too much to trust,
too much to live into,
too much to fall back onto?

I suppose we can laugh in derision or we can laugh in joyful hope. I suppose we can join the crowd chuckling at the door or we can listen for Jesus:

Don't be afraid, just believe...

Amen.

Fat Calves and New Teeth

LUKE 15:11–32

Porsha hollered, “Come on over here and sit down. I’ve got a testimony for you.”

She gave me a little kiss on the cheek, and I caught a whiff of stale cigarettes and sweet perfume. With her hair done up, her face made up, and her countenance lifted up, she gave me a big toothless grin, grabbed hold of my hand, and began to testify. She said, “I’ve been praying for years for my husband. I’ve been driving these people to their last nerve always praying for my husband.”

A shadow of confusion crossed over my face.
I’d known Porsha for years, and I’d never known her to be married.

She was a drug-addict-hooker.
She lived on the margins.
She surfaced at Roseland Christian Ministries (RCM) and lived in the shelter for women.
She helped fix meals for the homeless men.
She worked at RCM and moved into a house that RCM owned.
She was often the only woman in the circle of men at Morning Prayers.
She was colorful, charismatic, and always made me smile.

She said, "Twenty years ago I got married. He was a good man – always brought his check home and didn't mess around. But I started hanging out on the streets and got hooked on drugs. I left and lost him. Pretty soon I didn't even know where he was. That was 17 years ago. But we never got divorced; we've always been married. I just didn't know where he was."

The shadow on my face folded into a chuckle.
I never dreamed she was married.

She said, "But I been praying that I would find my sweet little husband. And then one day last week he came in the front door of the Center while I was walking out the back. Somebody told him I was in the alley. I was having a smoke, had my hat pulled down low, and he walked up and asked my name. Sweet Jesus! Seventeen years later my husband was standing right in front of me!"

Dear friends, take a deep breath and enjoy that moment.

Porsha continued, "God has been so good to me! You just don't know. We're going to have a recommitment service. I asked Reverend Tony if he would give us some counseling because 17 years is a big gap. He took me back before, but 17 years – whew! Sweet Jesus. I just thank God. I am so blessed!"

The chuckle on my face opened into astonishment.

> You don't think of addicts who spend years getting in and out of cars on South Michigan Avenue living happily ever after. You don't think of a marriage sustaining 17 years of separation. And yet, there sat Porsha with eyes bright, spirit buoyant, and smiling like it was Easter – with only two raggedy bent teeth left in her mouth.

She said, "He gets a disability check and Veteran's Benefits and we're looking for a house. He told me they have dentists at the VA, and I could get some teeth made. The street tore up my mouth, but I like to talk and I've got a lot to say, and it would be nice to get new teeth. God is good! I can't thank him enough for what he's done for me!"

Grab a new dress!
Put on your dancing shoes!
Kill the fatted calf and meet me at the *Why Not Lounge*!
The prodigal wife has been found!
The prodigal wife has come home!
Let the party begin!

Dear friends, in this world fairy tales and love stories include bumps and bruises that don't mend or heal easily. The journey home is hard, but the day after homecoming is just as hard. And yet, at that moment, history gave way to hope and in Porsha's heart forgiveness and love triumphed. Something that was dead was now alive. Thanks be to God!

There's no word in *The Parable of the Prodigal Son* about what happened after the party. The parable ends with the father and older son arguing in the front yard. We don't know if he went into the party or if he pouted on the porch. We don't know if the younger son lived a life of gratitude and testimony or if he got back on his feet and took off again. We don't know about the day after the homecoming…

> What we know is that when the younger son was walking back humiliated, hungry, and homesick, his father ran toward him, threw his arms around him, and threw a party.

Too often the parable is read about the boys.

There's the wayward son who spent his inheritance on fast cars, fast women, and ended up eating out of the bin behind the homeless shelter. There's the stiff-play-by-the-rules-sour-puss-brother who was angry because the score wasn't being kept. But the parable isn't necessarily about the character or comparison of the brothers.

What if the parable is about the Father?

What if the parable is about the party?

What if we read it this way?

The son comes to the father and asks what he would inherit if his father were dead. Then he takes the money and runs, leaving his dad for dead.

Only, he squanders his life. He blows it all and ends up a shell, a homeless shadow on the margins. Until one day he comes to his senses and realizes that whatever life he had is over. He's a dead man walking in a dead land.

So, he hatches a plan. I'm not suggesting that he wasn't sorry. I'm not suggesting that he wasn't repentant. But he schemes a reconstruction of the relationship. He may be dead as a son, but his father might be kind enough to take him back as a servant. So, if he's sorry, if he's good, if the books are still being kept, maybe he could negotiate a better situation than life on the street. And with that he turns for home.

His father sees him – teeth missing, hair nappy, stinking like a pig – but coming up the road. And before the boy can breathe a word, before he can voice his plan, before he can even say he's sorry…

His father hoists up his robe and runs like a little school girl toward him.

Without shame or hesitation,
without weighing the balance or checking the books,
without waiting for a confession,
the father gathers the son in his arms and bridges the gap with love and forgiveness. Let the party begin!

Robert Farrar Capon puts it this way:

> *The boy never gets his confession out until after the kiss, until after the embrace. Confession is not a pre-condition to forgiveness. It is something that you do after you know that you are forgiven. Confession is not something you do in order to get forgiveness. It is something you do in order to celebrate the forgiveness you got for nothing. Nobody can earn forgiveness...*

Dear friends, this isn't a cheeky comeback story about the boy with the courage to go home. This is a story of forgiveness undeserved. This isn't a story about someone finally getting it right. This is a story of finding a lost sheep, a lost coin, a dead son. This isn't a repentance story; this is a resurrection story!

Who knows how far down the road the father ran to kiss the son...
I'm not about to put boundaries or limitations around how far grace extends or God would go.
The dead father is alive!
The dead son is alive!

Paul puts it this way:

> *...because of his great love for us, God, who is rich in*

> *mercy made us alive with Christ, even when we were dead in transgressions – it is by grace you have been saved.*

The father has his son back.
The hooker has a husband.
The dead are alive.
Thanks be to God!

Of course, the other brother still thinks his life counts for something. He still believes that "deserve" has something to do with it. He's still convinced that somebody is keeping track. And he wants nothing to do with a party that includes his brother. He thinks his father shames the family by welcoming such a sinner.

The story ends there. With the father on the porch pleading with his son to come in for a glass of wine and a piece of bread. And, therein lies the scandal of the gospel.

Before we even knew we were dead
– God made us alive in Christ.
Before we got the words out of our mouths
– God made us alive in Christ.
Before we started to keep track
– God made us alive in Christ.
Before we spoke a word of confession
– God made us alive in Christ.

The only thing needed to get into the party is being dead.
Our only hope is resurrection.
We can wait on the porch with the brother until we die.
Or, we can acknowledge our death and come on in to the party.
It's big and messy and loud, but there is room enough for everyone.

So, whoever you are…
addict/alcoholic or "good Christian,"
whether you get lost in keeping track or you just lost track,
whatever teeth you're missing...
There's music playing.
The party's started.
The father is dancing with his child.
The bride is dancing with her husband.
Come to the table, there's bread and wine for everyone.

Thanks be to God.
Amen.

Kingdom Arithmetic

MATTHEW 18:21-35

How many times should you forgive?
How far would you go to forgive someone?

Consider the story of Alvin Straight…
At 73 years old, Alvin – a retired Iowa farmer with cataracts, bad hips, two canes, a propensity for bad cigars, and fourteen children, seven of whom survived – learned that his brother, Lyle, suffered a stroke on his farm in Mount Zion, Wisconsin. And although they were once as close as brothers could be, they hadn't spoken for more than a decade. They were estranged from one another with a chasm between them as wide as the Iowa sky.

So, afraid that life was reaching low ebb, with emphysema setting up shop in his lungs, Alvin acknowledged that the time to settle up accounts was running short. He said, "I want to sit with him and look up at the stars like we used to, long ago." And with that spirit, this crusty-old-codger climbed aboard the only thing he could still drive, his riding lawn mower, and he set out for Wisconsin.

The first lawnmower barely got him out of town before it broke down. So, Alvin had it towed home, shot it as if it were a horse, and then with his Social Security check bought a 1966 John Deere riding lawn mower. Towing a covered-trailer full of wieners and camping gear, he again turned his face to the east and headed for Wisconsin.

Puttering along the berm at a stately six miles an hour he traveled some three hundred miles across the top of Iowa. It was a slow journey. One doesn't drive a lawnmower to Wisconsin quickly. Alvin was on the road for five weeks – a geriatric knight on a quest with his trusty motorized steed as his only companion. He ventured forth to forgive and be forgiven…

Hollywood captured this story in the movie *The Straight Story*. They couldn't make up something so absurdly full of life and grace.

How many times should you forgive?
How far would you go to forgive someone?

In our text, bumbling-irrepressible-Peter asks Jesus the same: How far should I go? How many times should I forgive someone who sins against me?

What's often lost in the popular reading of this text is its context. Immediately preceding this exchange Jesus tells the parable of the sheepherder leaving the ninety-nine to search for the one last lost sheep, and then he offers a practical four-step process to settle disputes among his called-out-followers that ends with the offender being treated as if he or she was a "pagan or a tax collector." The same ones with whom Jesus shared meals and kept company.

Then, the very next thing Peter asks is, "How many times shall I forgive someone who sins against me?"

The text doesn't give any indication if this was all part of the same conversation or if Matthew is simply stacking up the teachings of Jesus regarding our common life. But again, even as God pursues us, Jesus offers a way of being that's rooted in a different allegiance, that turns things on their heads, that seems outlandish, irrational, inconceivable. If the preceding text is Jesus at his practical best, this is Jesus at his impractical worst.

Because, when Peter – proud as can be – asks about forgiveness and suggests the fullness of seven times, he thinks he's scoring points with Jesus. Only to be trumped by the absurdity of seventy-seven or seventy-seven times seven.

Jesus responds with a figure of speech that suggests something beyond what we can count, and in doing so references the memory of Lamech. In Genesis 4, Lamech (a descendent of the murderer, Cain) boasts to his wives of his code of revenge. In his words:

> *I have killed a man for wounding me, a young man for injuring me.*
> *If Cain is avenged seven times, then Lamech seventy times seven.*

Lamech offers the arithmetic of the world: An eye for eye and a tooth for a tooth, a pound of flesh for an ounce of offense. Lamech would go to untold ends to settle the score. If wronged, he would get even. His would be the last word. But Jesus turns the tables on Peter, on Lamech, on all of us...

Rather than balance the books unlimited times, Jesus commands his followers to forgive unlimited times. Rather than grab for revenge, Jesus commands his disciples to offer forgiveness. The followers of Jesus are to be so generous of spirit as to forgive beyond their ability to count. Jesus offers the arithmetic of the Kingdom.

But that has to be hyperbole, doesn't it?

Jesus can't mean forgiveness for the really hard and hurtful stuff in life. He must be talking about the petty offenses that happen among believers: rudeness, gossip, a mean word, a cold shoulder. He doesn't give us a process or guidelines for how to be reconciled.

Surely, he's not talking about forgiveness for dictators or terrorists.

Surely, he's not suggesting forgiveness of the abuser.

Surely, he's talking about forgiveness for those already forgiven.

Right?

Imagine the cloud that crossed Peter's face. He thought he was going to impress Jesus – only to be staggered by the jaw-dropping absurdity of forgiveness beyond measure.

So, Jesus, seeing the trouble in Peter's face, launches into a colorful cartoon where the circumstances and scales are overblown.

The king was keeping books and the servant owed something like a bazillion dollars. The servant offers to pay it back on time. Think: a dollar a day on the national debt. He might as well drive a lawn mower from Iowa to the southern tip of Argentina.

> Except, the king looks with mercy on the man and forgives his debt. Scott free. Every last penny. Wiped clean. Good to go. No interest, no points, no penalties, no threats, no recrimination, no keeping track. Free! Thanks be to God.

Dear friends, we have all been wronged.

And any tension or expectation in a sermon about forgiveness is lost because we know the ending – we're supposed to forgive. But we also know that there are hurts too deep, evil too profound, and the demands for revenge or justice are limitless. So, the words of Jesus seem like pious platitudes that don't take into account the real world.

Tom Long writes that the parable is about proportion. In his words:

> *When one gets a sense of proportion, a sense of the size of our sinful debt and the immensity of God's mercy, then no one would dare attempt to ration forgiveness. We know too well that the little boat in which we are sailing is floating on a deep sea of grace and that forgiveness is not dispensed with an eyedropper but a fire hose.*

It is a wonderful image. The mercy of God is beyond our measure; who, then, are we to squeeze out forgiveness only when our standards are met, and our needs are satisfied, and our books are balanced?

I've lost track of how many weddings I've done. Sometimes I'll see a young couple, and I can't remember if I did their wedding or not. But, in my mushy memory there are moments of great humor and beauty that stand out.

One of those moments was a wedding in Holland, Michigan, in which the bride's cousin read a portion of I Corinthians 13. Typical wedding fare, except the cousin was a young Korean boy with Down Syndrome. He was nervous. His speech was halting. The words were hard to understand. He couldn't have been any cuter. His heart was wide open. And, he read:

Love keeps no record of wrongs.

There wasn't a dry eye in the room.

Dear friends, what if forgiveness isn't really about number or distance? What if forgiveness isn't about arithmetic? To count, to keep track, isn't really forgiveness.

Forgiveness isn't waiting for a final ledger.
Forgiveness isn't holding the IOU, waiting to balance the books.
Forgiveness isn't burying the hatchet, but putting a marker on the site.
Forgiveness is limitless because it doesn't keep track.

Love keeps no record of wrongs.

If we're loved and forgiven by God, with our sins erased on a cross, isn't it possible that others are too? And as God's love in Christ keeps no record of our wrongs, isn't it possible that we would see others with a similar generosity?

Debt is really about power.

If I hold you in debt, I hold power over you. And forgiveness, therefore, is about giving up power, letting go of the upper hand. In forgiving we make ourselves vulnerable, we give up self for the sake of the other, for the sake of the relationship, for the sake of love.

Alvin Straight was finally moved by love.

There was no rehashing of wrongs.

There was no tit for tat.

There was no scramble for the last winning word.

There was the simple recognition that finally forgiveness is wider than the Iowa sky. And at the end of the journey, two brothers sat on the porch and looked up at the stars, and you would want to make the night last forever.

So, this morning we're reminded that the grace and love of God forgives sin beyond measure. And, as that is true…

Maybe there's a lawnmower we can start up.

Maybe there's a sister or a brother we can forgive.

Maybe there's a debt we can release.

Maybe there's a baby we can baptize.

Amen.

Wearing Down God

LUKE 18:1-8

There is an iconic scene in *Family Guy* – the bawdy animated sitcom. Stewie, the baby with the football-shaped-head, toddles up to Lois, his mother. She's sitting on the bed, exhausted and staring straight ahead. Stewie says,

> *Lois. Lois. Lois. Mom. Mom. Mom. Mom. Mommy. Mommy. Mommy. Mommy. Ma. Ma. Ma. Ma. Mum. Mum. Mum. Mummy. Mummy. Momma. Momma...*

Finally, Lois whirls around and yells, "What?"
To which Stewie replies, "Hi!" and runs out of the room giggling.

The genius of that scene is that we all know the incessant, insistent demands of a child. We've experienced the relentless requests that eventually wear down even the strongest among us. Annoying or endearing, we know the voice of one who won't give up.

And that seems to be what Jesus wants.
Pray like that.
Pray with persistence.
Pray with insistence.
Pray like Stewie.

Pray like the widow.

For even a corrupt judge will eventually give in and say, "Yes." How much more the one who created you and calls you his own? If that bloke eventually crumbles and answers the widow's request – just imagine what your Heavenly Father will do!

Maybe that's all there is to this parable. As Luke puts it:

Then Jesus told his disciples a parable to show them that they should always pray and not give up.

This isn't a puzzling parable or a colorful story with a surprising twist. This isn't the way of the world turned on its head. This is a direct volley – a clear shot. Pray without ceasing, and never lose heart. And maybe that's enough. To use Jesus' language from a few chapters earlier:

Ask and it will be given to you; seek and you will find, knock and the door will be opened...

Who can argue with that? Surely not the women who gather at Hope to pray on the first Monday of every month...

There's a team of women who meet here to pray. With tenacity and tenderness, they pray for the church, for our children, and for our seniors. They pray for babies in the womb and those grieving the death of loved ones. They pray for the sick and the suffering. They pray in joy, they pray in sorrow, and they've been doing it for years! They pray for you. They're a living embodiment of this parable. Thanks be to God.

Therefore, let's make this a short sermon. Let's heed this call and pray up a storm. Let's beat a path to God's door and keep pounding until our knuckles bleed. For, surely God will answer. Around you sit those who can bear witness to persistence in prayer. Again, thanks be to God.

And yet…

And yet, there's something unsettling here.

What of the family that prays faithfully for years only to watch a loved one waste away in the stench of chemo and cancer? What of the couple struggling with infertility? How many prayers for how long? What of the longsuffering prayers that the scourge of gun violence will not take one more child's life? What of the parent praying for a child who can't shake the black dog of depression? How many prayers for how long?

Do we just hang those prayers on the knowledge that God is answering – just not the answer that we're longing for, praying for, waiting for, or pleading for? Is it a matter of effort and we need to knock longer and louder? Maybe it has to do with us…

Dear friends, is that all scripture has to offer? Prayer as a divine slot machine that responds to those who keep putting in nickels. Surely prayer is something more than waiting for God to fix things on our behalf. Surely there must be something more than the instruction to pester God until God finally answers our prayer…

Then Jesus told his disciples a parable to show them that they should always pray and not give up.

What are we to make of this parable?

Does it turn on God being more generous than a mid-level magistrate? Is it about the plucky persistence of the widow? Is this about the nature of faith or the nature of God? Is it a rallying call to storm the gates of heaven and a challenge to those of us who are lollygagging on the spiritual sidelines? What are we to make of this parable?

Maybe this is helpful...

The widow in the parable is emblematic of the most vulnerable and voiceless in society. Widows had few rights. Their late husband's property was transferred right through them to their closest male relative. Their status was determined by their relationship to a man.

But the courts made space for widows. Old Testament law required judges to listen to their concerns. That requirement was only superseded by the needs of orphans.

So, this judge – no matter how puffed up with pride – was obligated to listen to the widow. He could have been dismissive, he could have been distracted, but rightfully this widow would not be shuffled to the side. And therefore...

she kept after him,
she kept crying out,
she kept demanding to be heard,
she kept pleading her case,
until he gave in.

Quite frankly, the Greek here is more colorful than our English translation. The judge finally folds, saying,

> *I will see that she gets justice so that she won't eventually come and give me a black eye...*

The sense of the word "attack" (our translation) is that of striking one under the eye. The judge wasn't compassionate to the widow's circumstances; he was worried about her left hook. He didn't want to explain the shiner to the barristers around the bar, so he hears her case and grants her justice.

We should also note that this parable only appears in Luke's gospel, and it comes hot on the heels of Jesus talking about the end of the age. He says to his disciples:

> *I tell you, on that night two people will be in one bed; one will be taken and the other left. Two women will be grinding grain together; one will be taken and the other left. "Where Lord?" they asked. He replied, "Where there is a dead body there the vultures will gather."*

Gulp! Yikes! Shiver!

And with that, Jesus takes a deep breath and launches into this peculiar point-blank-parable about prayer…

Maybe it's helpful to remember that Luke wrote his gospel some twenty years after Jesus. And at that time, the followers of Jesus were trying to make sense of his life, death, and resurrection while hanging on to the extraordinary promise that he would return. A return they expected to be imminent.

But as they waited, and Jesus didn't come back, they became discouraged and dismayed. They lost heart. There was a Roman boot on their necks. They knew suffering and abuse. Justice seemed a long way off, and a promise delayed felt like a promise betrayed. So, it was easy to be disillusioned, disenchanted, and despairing. How long do we keep singing that "the world's about to turn"?

Dear friends, there's an eschatological dimension to this parable.
I'm not sure that it amounts to the simple equation: prayer equals effort multiplied by time. I'm not sure the encouragement is to just keep bringing your to-do list to God because eventually God will give in and release the storehouses of heaven.
This is about the longing for that day when widows and orphans will receive justice. This is about that day when peace will prevail. This is about that day when a table will be spread for all. This is about that day when God will make his dwelling with people, and the very hand of God will wipe away the last tear – for the old order of things has passed away.

And so, maybe, this parable is not so much instruction about how to pray as it is a picture of God granting justice and putting the world to rights. Maybe this parable is not so much about our persistence in prayer as it is about God's unrelenting faithfulness to his promises.

Therefore, don't lose heart. Don't give up faith. Keep praying – for that day is surely coming when justice and mercy will kiss.

Then Jesus told his disciples a parable to show them that they should always pray and not give up.

As one scholar puts it:

When justice seems far off, we pray. When rejection is near at hand, we pray. We persist in praying for what is right. We keep our hearts focused on the coming kingdom and its characteristics. In the face of injustice, we do the right thing and pray for God to show himself as the just judge who makes peace and punishment as it should be.

It strikes me that belief in God is relatively easy. Most people believe in God – an anonymous, amorphous deity, distant and mysterious. And worship of that God may even have its own culturally conditioned beauty: the language of liturgy, the glory of singing, choral music beautifully rendered, the smells and bells, the silence. Even sitting with a circle of church friends has its own goodness. Belief or worship of God is doable. But prayer?

Prayer gives that vague God a certain name and a particular urgency. Prayer is the comforting or confounding recognition that God has personhood. Prayer is the faith – even the size of a mustard seed – that God "is."

And while the actual form of prayer may be incidental, any prayer that has even a shred of authenticity, hopes or believes that God can or will act. And prayer, therefore, is finally longing for God's will, God's way, and God's justice and mercy in this world.

Dear friends, may our lives be marked by faithful enduring prayer. May we be among those who are found faithful – still praying in the dawning light of that great morning when Jesus shall return to answer every prayer we've ever whispered.

Amen.

An Accounting

MARK 12:38–44

I sat next to a saint. With hands wrinkled and bruised by life, she fidgeted with the tubes, wires, and the edge of her hospital gown. We talked about the results of a recent test and the next steps ordered by the doctor. Her spirit was buoyant, and she was eager to get home.

She'd lived a long, rich life.
She married and buried a husband.
She had children and grandchildren and great-grandchildren.
She lived her whole life in the shelter of the church.
She knew the heartbreak of a child dying.
She knew her greatest comfort was that she was not her own but belonged…

I sat next to a saint but even saints have issues, and eventually our conversation swung to broken family relationships. She said, "I tell them that one day they will have to give an accounting." And a few minutes later she added, "One day they will be called to give an account, and God will punish as he sees fit."

I said, "Our faith is that God is merciful and forgiving."

"Yes, but you still have to give an account."

"Well… we're all in trouble if God is counting."

She laughed, "Some of us will have more to answer for than others."

Embedded deep in us is the idea that God is keeping track –
that he's making a list and checking it twice,
that there's a giant spreadsheet in the sky,
that God will hold us accountable for what we did, what we squandered, what we saved, and how we behaved.
Because surely this life counts for something, and we'll all have to give an account.

Dear friends, given that cosmology, the widow who gave her last two bits is a saint.

She gave everything that she had. The Greek word here is a form of *bios* – from which we get biology. She gave her very life. In the middle of the religious marketplace, above the din of the wealthy getting their names etched in the temple bricks, against the backdrop of fancy-pants-preachers in flowing robes, from out of her poverty, this anonymous widow held nothing back and gave her bottom dollar.

And Jesus sees her. Everyone else has passed her over, but Jesus pays attention and points her out. She becomes a living sermon illustration.

In an online sermon – made to be pilfered, plagiarized, and preached in pulpits all across America – one preacher puts it this way:

> *Jesus takes an opportunity in the passage before us to point out an unlikely person – a poor widow – as an example of what God values most in the stewardship of our money. I want to suggest that what Jesus values in this woman are a Genuine Heart, a Grateful Spirit, and a Generous Attitude.*

Maybe that's the point. Maybe this text is meant to encourage us to give genuinely, gratefully, and generously. For God is watching. Whoever you are, wherever you are, with whatever you have…

It's not the measure that you give;
it's the measure that you have left.
It's not about the fortune in the world's eyes;
it's the fortune in God's eyes.
It's not about giving in our wealth;
it's about giving in our poverty.
Maybe this widow and her two coins is a model for all of us.
Because, after all, there will be an accounting.

Dear friends, maybe there's a different way to read this text.

There's nothing here to suggest the tone of Jesus' voice. There's nothing to suggest that when Jesus called over the disciples to point out the widow his instructions were, "Remember the rich young ruler? Well, look at how this poor widow does what he couldn't do or wouldn't do. Be like the widow. Go thou and do thee likewise…"

There is no indication that his intention was praise.
What if there was a tone of sadness to his voice?
What if there was lament?

What if he points her out in admiration but also
in astonishment?
What if this is not about accounting but about revolution?

Consider...

Jesus had just arrived in Jerusalem and was creating quite a stir. He was turning things upside down. In the face of Roman authority, he was welcomed as a king – albeit riding on a donkey. In the place of business as usual he started a wild rumpus in the temple – overturning tables and driving out the moneychangers. When questioned by the chief priests and elders, he unsettled their authoritative grip. And all of this was being done in the shadow of the coming cross. Nothing was what it seemed...

A whole new world was being born,
a whole new way of keeping track was being revealed,
a whole new kingdom was coming.

And then in the middle of the temple, Jesus points out the powerful and the pompous parading around, perpetrating a system that preyed on the poor. He calls out the ruling religious elites and the long pray-ers who think that a score is being kept. He names a temple practice that exploited widows for profit and positioned priests between God and people.

Jesus then sat down opposite the temple treasury box. Or, maybe better said, as Jesus sat down in opposition to the treasury box, Jesus saw one of these widows coming.

She silently slips in her temple tax.
She pays her part.
She does the only thing that she knows to do.
There will be an accounting.
She throws in her life.

Barbara Brown Taylor asks:

> *Are we really supposed to admire a woman who gave her last cent to a morally bankrupt religious institution? Was it right for her to surrender her living to those who lived better than her? What if she were someone you knew, someone of limited means, who decided to send her last dollar to the 700 Club? Would that be admirable or scandalous? Would it be a good deed or a crying shame?*

Dear friends, as Jesus points out the discrepancy between the teachers of the law and the poor widow, what if he's turning the temple on its head? What if he's establishing a new way of counting?

> The temple system of sacrifice, the social structures that support injustice, and the corrupted covenant – were all coming down. While it's true that Jesus doesn't chastise the woman for participating in the system, neither does he praise her. And, in the next verses, Mark records Jesus predicting the destruction of the temple. It was all coming down by way of the cross. Jesus was dismantling an accounting system.

Don't count on religious observance and temple tax.
Don't trust in long prayers or November stewardship campaigns.
Don't put your faith in accounting.
Don't bank on what you do…

> Trust in the one who is turning this world around.
> Trust in the one who would give his life.
> Trust in the one who clears the books.

While in Israel I went to the Dead Sea. Without even a hint of a cloud, it was 115 degrees. But it was a dry heat…

The trip was drawing to a close, and I'd reached my fill of seeing caves where something biblical might have happened, so I hurried down to the water. They gave us an hour. I was going to spend every minute of it in the Dead Sea.

There were people from all over the world floating in the water and slathering on the black mud that's supposed to have therapeutic powers. I ran into the water like a kid let out of school for summer vacation…

But! The water wasn't cool; it was hot. It wasn't refreshing; it was thick, salty, acidic, and it burned anything tender. You couldn't sink or swim to save your soul. You could only float. I bobbed and sizzled on top of the water like an egg on a griddle.

Earl Simmons, a pastor from a storefront church in Washington, D.C., didn't know how to swim. So, he sat sweating in the shade along the shore until we cajoled and coaxed him into the water. It took the better part of an hour, but finally he came into the water. Once in, with fear and trembling, he grunted, groaned, flapped, and sputtered, and… And the more he struggled and splashed, the more he stirred up a frenzy that made no difference. But when he realized that the water was going to hold him,

when he learned that he wasn't going to sink,
when he relaxed and let his arms and legs rest,
when he simply fell back into the buoyancy,
then a giant smile crossed his face and he cried out,
"Hallelujah! I'm swimming! I'm swimming!
Thank you, Jesus! Thank you, Jesus!"
And he laughed and laughed, deep and long.

Faith is counting on Christ. With nothing else to add, nothing else to do, nothing else to give but our poverty, faith is falling back into God's unfailing grip. The only accounting is God in Christ.

In the words of Craig Dykstra:

> *Faith is the knowledge of the reality of God's buoyancy – of God's upholding love and mercy, present to the world and to us all in every situation and circumstance of life. Faith is life lived resting in God's grace.*

Dear friends, no matter how broke or broken you are,
no matter how salty or acidic this old world gets,
no matter how our relationships falter or our bodies fail,
no matter how rough the water or how dead the sea,
we belong, body and soul, in life and in death,
to our faithful Savior Jesus Christ.

The Apostle Paul puts it this way:

> *For you know the grace of our Lord Jesus Christ, that though he was rich, yet for our sake he became poor, so that through his poverty we might become rich.*

That's the only accounting that matters.
Thanks be to God.
Amen.

Through the Dung Gate

JOHN 19:16–22

Chances are that Jesus came into Jerusalem through the Dung Gate.

The south end of Jerusalem is a steady steep slope. Sewage flowed down that slope and out of the city. The Dung Gate is at the base of that hill, and garbage was taken out through that entrance to be burned outside the city walls. The south end was toxic, smelly, and unsanitary. And in the grand tradition of environmental injustice, the south end was where the poor folks lived. The south end was the most densely populated part of the city. The south end was where most of the Hebrews lived.

Chances are that Jesus came into Jerusalem through the Dung Gate.

While it probably didn't resemble the sunny, sanitized parades of Sunday school flannel graphs, Jesus rustled up a donkey and entered Jerusalem by way of the ghetto. He was greeted by crowds looking for a leader to overthrow the Roman occupation. Longing for a messiah to establish the Kingdom of God, they welcomed him by waving palm branches and shouting old songs of hope and triumph.

Dear friends, Jesus begins the last week of his life
at the base of that south side hill,
at the bottom of the toilet,
and from there he stirs up a stink storm in the temple court.

The temple is set atop that slope. A massive structure, the temple courtyard would have been full of vendors, soldiers, slaves, money changers, and animals. And, it is entirely conceivable that as Jesus came up from the south, he would have headed to the temple courtyard, caused a ruckus, and set into motion the events that led to his crucifixion on Friday.

John writes that Jesus was arrested in a garden on the other side of the Kidron Valley. That valley is on the east side of the city. It's a steep but not very deep gully that runs about twenty miles and falls some four thousand feet towards the Dead Sea. The temple is on one side; the garden of Gethsemane is on the other. Judas and the company of soldiers would have crossed the valley, grabbed Jesus, and escorted him into the city through one of the north end gates – where the rich people lived. Where they would encounter Caiaphas, Herod Antipas, and Pilate.

So, from Sunday to Friday Jesus goes
from the Dung Gate to the seat of power,
from the backend of the outhouse to the edge of the throne,
from the bottom of the social ladder to the top rung
of the empire.

Our text picks up with Jesus being led out to the crucifixion site. There's a variety of traditions and lots of scholarly speculation, but there's no clarity about the actual place where

Jesus was crucified. What is clear is that crucifixion was a familiar practice.

The Romans didn't invent crucifixion, but they certainly made it their own as a way to maintain order over subjects and slaves.

For example, historians record that about a hundred years before Jesus, Spartacus led a slave revolt that ended in a bloody battle and "6,000 of his followers were crucified along the 130 or so miles of the Appian Way from Rome to Capua, making it roughly one cross every 40 yards" (N.T Wright). Or, the historian Josephus describes a revolt in Galilee led by Judas ben Hezekiah in which Varus, the Roman general, puts down the uprising and crucifies about 2,000 of the rebels.

You get the point. Crucifixion was a tool of the empire to crush rebellions and snuff out hope. Death on a cross could take days, and the bodies were left hanging to be picked over by vermin and buzzards and to serve as a reminder…

When we read Jesus say, "Take up your cross and follow…" it seems like a metaphorical call to discipleship, but we have no idea how patently absurd that would have sounded to first century Jews who saw their fathers and brothers brutalized by the empire's apparatus of torture.

John writes that Jesus takes up his cross and carries it to where he is crucified. Again, what stands out is the common-mundane-nothing-specialness…

John doesn't offer any gory details. The crucifixion is told in the three words of a subordinate clause. It would be hard to be less dramatic. John writes that Jesus is crucified with two others.

...one on each side and Jesus in the middle.

I know the symbolism here is that Jesus is placed in the middle of human life. This is a Christocentric picture. This is Jesus at the crux of human history, the hinge upon which creation's redemption swings.

But let us not lose sight that Jesus takes his place between two nameless, faceless criminals. Jesus takes his place between two families that will be forever ruptured by loss. Jesus takes his place between two more who are tossed aside by the empire. Who knows what they did or didn't do? Who cares? In a culture of mass incarceration and capital punishment their lives barely matter. And there's Jesus, smack dab in the middle.

Pilate has a sign affixed to the cross of Jesus: *Jesus of Nazareth, the King of the Jews.* And in doing so, Pilate writes the first gospel.

Eventually there will be oceans of ink spilled about Jesus, but these are the first words, this is the first written line. It tells who he is, where he came from, and what he did for work. Almost everything you need to know is in those few words – except for the deity or divinity part. As one writer puts it, this is "the Gospel according to Pilate." And Pilate has it written in the three major languages of the known world. This is meant to be a universal proclamation. This is so the world may know...

Historians believe that, in part, crucifixion was a taunt. If those who led uprisings thought that they were rising up, well, here you go...

We'll raise you up.
We'll raise you high up for all to see.
We'll raise you high up on this cross.
And so, Pilate raises Jesus up with a title over his head:
King of the Jews.
But the Chief Priests will have none of it. They want the wording changed. They know they're being mocked as well.

As C.K. Barrett puts it:

> *The Jew's objection to the sign was natural. In the first place, they had just declared that they had no king but Caesar, and the sign, if they accept it, was tantamount to an admission of sedition; and in the second place, to suggest that a powerless, condemned, and dying outcast was the king of their nation was a studied insult.*

Pilate lets it stand.
And Pilate's not wrong…
Jesus is from Nazareth, and he is an extension of David's throne, the King of Jews. Only this king now joins the ranks of those "fettered, spat upon, naked" and executed by the state.

Let's stop right there.

A thoughtful young woman who was raised in the church said to me recently, "I don't get why Christians are so strict about Jesus. There is nothing wrong with meditation, spirituality, Buddhism, and centering in the moment. I mean, it's all about love and being your best self. And Jesus is part of that, but I don't get why they're so strict about Jesus."

She gives voice to the hearts and thoughts of many.

> Faith is pragmatic. What matters is what makes our lives healthier, happier, and more whole. So, Jesus is part of a panoply of options, a help, a means to an end. And church fits into that same spiritual toolbox. What matters is how church makes us feel, what gifts it gives us for living, what relationships it helps us form, what it does for us…

I'm not going to argue with or belittle that. In fact, the gospel of John reads that the very Son of God descended from the heights of heaven because he so loves us. Jesus knows the way from God and the way back to God. Jesus came to embody the love of God. Let us be our best loving selves. What's wrong with that?

Again. I'm not going to argue with or belittle that.
There are all sorts of ways to grapple with God in Christ.
One could do a lot worse.

But the patently absurd and staggering mystery is that the journey of Jesus was unto death. Jesus embodying the love of God meant crucifixion. It meant being abandoned, mocked, whipped, and suffering what was the lowest, most horrific death of the day.

That's a far cry from anything pragmatic.
That's a far cry from anything healthy, happy, and whole.
That's a far cry from being your best self.

If God in Christ is nailed to the cross, I'm not sure that I can just relegate that to one more entrée in a spiritual smorgasbord. The crucifixion rightly drops us in our tracks. Takes away our breath. To sit with the cross too long is to be left speechless…

So, we are quick to talk about what the crucifixion accomplishes. We are quick to fill the silence with theories about how the death of Jesus pays a price, or satisfies a wrath, or makes things right. We want to answer the questions with an explanation that makes sense. We want something that fits in our tool box.

And yet, dear friends, at least for today, I can't.

I can't explain the descent of God from heaven's throne, to the bottom of a poop-stained hill, to being crucified on a blood-stained plot of land. I can't make it more plausible, palatable, or pretty. I can't make it less monstrous or mysterious. I'm sure there is a time for reflection and theologizing about what "plan" being nailed to a cross fulfilled, but at least for today, I am left with the silence of Pilate.

What is written is written.

I can only confess that if love prompted God to descend in Christ, then there is

love enough for everyone broken and bruised,
love enough for everyone grieving and lost,
love enough for everyone abandoned and addicted,
for everyone stuck in self-loathing or bloated with self-love,
love enough for everyone stuck on death row.

If love prompted God in Christ to descend to death, then there is love enough for me, and you, and my young friend. If love prompted God in Christ to descend to death – even death on a cross – then let us join God in exalting him

...to the highest place and give him the name that is above every name, that at the name of Jesus every knee

> *should bow, in heaven and on earth and under the earth, and every tongue confess, that Jesus Christ is Lord, to the glory of God the Father.*

Amen.

Hanging on Two Nails

MATTHEW 22:34-46

Darwin looked like a hobbit. I don't mean in a vaguely familiar way – as one might look like a giraffe or a goat or a golden retriever. I mean, he seriously looked like a hobbit.

Darwin was short of stature with bowed legs and a barrel chest that sunk down into his belly. His face was framed by a wispy white beard – no mustache, just a thin white line to frame his round face, bulbous nose, and bright eyes. He often wore a floppy sailor's cap atop his bald head, and he always ambled along with a certain vigor, as if there was important business to which he must attend.

Darwin and his wife – who also looked like a hobbit – lived in the foothills of the Adirondack Mountains. They were hill people. They had a beautiful plot of land on which they raised honey bees, heated with a woodstove, powered with solar, and made mead. They were sturdy, self-reliant, and delightful.

Darwin was quick to speak his mind. And while there could be a twinkle in his eyes, they were just as quick to flash with anger. He was as stubborn as he was stout. He was a research engineer and was pretty sure he was right about most things, but he was very clear about religion. Religion was simple. It all boiled down to one thing: Love God and love your neighbor.

Everything else was extraneous.
Everything else was window dressing.
Everything else was speculation.

Darwin thought that the rule of love was the core truth of all religions. Anything added was added at our peril because it was myth or murkiness. Anything else was human ritual, regulation, or rules that cluttered up the truth.

Therefore, given this position, Darwin wouldn't join in a litany for the confession of sin. He wasn't going to confess something that he didn't do. And he wouldn't recite the Apostle's Creed. He wasn't going to say something that was manufactured religious mumbo-jumbo. He wasn't going to say something that was outside of his rational framework. He was simply going to live by the rule of love.

There was a simple beauty to Darwin's perspective. He had religion honed down to what really matters. And Jesus trimmed it down to the same.

Love God with everything you've got
– your heart, your soul, your mind.
And love your neighbor as yourself.

Jesus and a hobbit have religion in a nutshell...
Or, is there something more?

Our text this morning is the last in a series of questions posed to Jesus by the political-religious class. Matthew stacks them up like waves crashing on the beach. First came the disciples of the Pharisees and the Herodians, then they're followed by the Sadducees, and finally the Pharisees themselves roll up.

The first wave was a question about paying taxes to Caesar. They were trying to catch Jesus with treason or heresy.

The second wave was a question about a widow who was married seven times and who she would be married to at the resurrection. They were trying to catch him in speculation about something that they didn't believe in.

The third wave was this question about the greatest commandment. The word translated here as "test" is the same word used when Satan tempts or tests Jesus at the beginning of Matthew's gospel.

This was no *colloquium doctum*.
This was no friendly theological discourse.
This was an exchange with everything hanging in the balance.

The Pharisees huddled together, selected their most distinguished legal scholar, and sent him to Jesus with their cleverly crafted question. They slid up with a slick confidence. They thought they had Jesus cornered. If every law is from God, how would a mere mortal have any standing or wisdom to rank them?

To give evidence of the musical theater of my childhood, I'm reminded of the Hungarian phonetician in *My Fair Lady* trying to discern who Eliza Doolittle was and where she came from. In Henry Higgins' words:

Oozing charm from ev'ry pore,
He oiled his way around the floor.
Ev'ry trick that he could play,
He used to strip her mask away.

And when at last the dance was done,
He glowed as if he knew he'd won!

The Pharisees think they've won. They think they've stripped Jesus down to some disposable size. But…

But what if this is more than just a tricky final exam question?
What if there is more here than an attempt to trap Jesus?
What if it gets at an honest human question?

As a high school teacher, I grew weary of the query, "Do we need to know this for the test?" But in a moral universe we want to know the standards and expectations. We want to know the height of the bar. And, truth be told, our working list of life's rules and regulations is an amalgam of culture, family habit, religious tradition, and personal history…

In response to the question, "Will it be on the test?" the answer has ranged from and included:

No card playing or movie going.
No lawn mowing or going out to eat on Sunday.
No dancing, drinking, or dating girls that do.
For some, pacifism; for others, enlisted patriotism.
For some, church twice on Sundays;
  for others, 4:00 on a Saturday.
For some, heterosexuals only; for others, all are welcome.
For some, Christian education; for others, the public sphere.

You get the idea. Our guideposts are experienced through a particular cultural framework. That's not to suggest that they aren't true, worthy, or faithful, but they are also a unique expression of culture and context.

And, therefore, this question is more than just a way to jam up Jesus. It's more than an idle rabbinical game. It's a crucial question:

What's the essence of what we are supposed to do?
What's the greatest commandment?

Jesus responds with a startling simplicity. He quotes what they already know. He reaches back to the core of Hebrew scripture and offers a portion of the *Shema* of Deuteronomy 6:

> *Hear, O Israel: The Lord our God, the Lord is one. Love the Lord your God with all your heart and with all your soul and with all your strength...*

Jesus answers with part of a prayer that every practicing Jew would recite each morning and every evening. And then for good measure he tacks on a text from Leviticus 19. As you love God you would love that which bears the image of God.

Love God.
Love neighbor.
Somewhere there's a little hobbit dancing a jig.

Dear friends, there was really nothing earthshaking in the answer Jesus offered. In fact, in the Gospel of Luke, Jesus poses a similar question to a lawyer, and he responds with the same answer. Jesus is not breaking substantial new theological ground here. He's not offering a radical reconfiguration of truth.

He simply hangs all the law on two nails: Love of God and love of neighbor. The formula is memorable and its simplicity appealing.

Everything hangs on,

is connected to,
finds coherence,
or has meaning
in those two nails.

I know a young woman who tends bar – over-dyed jet-black hair, husky-smoky voice, a few tattoos, a little rough around the edges. Recently she began to date a gentleman caller. She liked him initially. He was a good guy who had a job, treated her decently, and went to church. All the basics. She was hopeful.

But then he began to question and critique her decisions and patterns. He began to talk of God's displeasure with her. She had second thoughts about him, began to avoid his advances, and refused his calls.

Finally, he simply texted her a biblical text. She asked me about the text because she wanted to know what it said, but she couldn't remember what text. "It was either John 14:15 or John 15:14…"

I am not sure it would have mattered.

John 14:15 "If you love me, you will obey what I command."
John 15:14 "You are my friends if you do what I command."

And therein lies the rub!

Jewish scholars count 631 laws in the *Torah*, and when Jesus answers the Pharisees, he's not dismissing or diminishing any of those laws. He's simply saying that they all hang on two nails. Pull out one of those nails and it all falls apart. In the words of John Calvin:

Surely the first foundation of righteousness is the worship (love) of God. When this is overthrown, all the remaining

> *parts of righteousness, like pieces of a shattered and fallen building, are mangled and scattered…*

Love is love as it lives into the law.
Love finds meaning not in good feelings but in obedience.
Love finds expression in how we live with God and neighbor.
Or, as Cornell West – African American scholar and raconteur – puts it:

> *Justice is love in public.*

Most good sermons would end there with the encouragement to live in love by obeying the commandments. And Jesus could have dropped that bit of biblical wisdom on the Pharisees and walked out the door leaving them feeling sort of foolish, but instead Jesus turns the tables and asks about the Messiah.

Matthew – in this most Jewish of gospels – includes an odd little exchange about the line of David and the coming of the Messiah. And this is the last time in which the political-religious class engage Jesus in discourse to catch him as some manner of fraud. They seem to have heard enough; now the plot moves to crucifixion.

But what if this odd little addendum is also a way to say that this is what love finally and fully looks like?

> This is love embodied. This is the greatest commandment expressed in flesh and blood. This is love of God and neighbor expressed not in pen and paper but in person. This is love hanging on two nails.

William Willimon puts it this way:

> *Jesus will give definition to all of this, not standing before the temple and having a theological argument, but by stretching out his arms on the cross.*

May we proclaim this morning, in the glorious light of that mystery…

That love hangs on,
is connected to,
finds coherence,
and has meaning
in Jesus Christ on the cross.

May our lives be modeled and marked by that love.
May our lives hang on that love.

Amen.

In Conversation with Criminals

LUKE 23:32–43

My grandmother, Winifred Amelia Smith, was a stout, stately English woman. From the head of the table, while pouring tea and serving short bread, she was easily mistaken for the Queen-mum. Pious, Bible-believing, and Plymouth Brethren, she lived to be 98.

During the last days of my grandmother's life, with family at her bedside, she memorably prayed, "O Lord, you saved the thief on the cross; surely you can save a sinner such as I…"

It was probably just a common prayer phrase – a line that she heard prayed over and over again. Something akin to "give them traveling mercies on their homeward way," or "Lord we just wanna pray…" But it's also emblematic of the way in which this conversation between Christ and two criminals has shaped the faith and imagination of God's people.

So this morning, as we close another year on the church calendar and celebrate Christ the King, we listen for the voice of God in conversation with criminals. In doing so, may our faith and our imaginations be so shaped and encouraged.

Crucifixion was common in first century Palestine.

> As a deterrent the Roman Empire crucified people on the hills outside of town or alongside the roads leading into town. Everyone knew what crucifixion looked like, smelled like, and sounded like – long slow suffering, lost control of bodily function, thirst, suffocation, a naked agony. It was an obscene, unspeakable horror meant to strip away any last vestige of humanity.

All four gospels recount Jesus being crucified between two criminals. Historians write that they weren't "common criminals." For while the Romans were a cruel-occupying-force, they didn't crucify people for shoplifting sandals or fudging on taxes. It's more likely that these criminals posed a threat to the empire – violent thugs, insurrectionists, terrorists. The word here in Luke for "criminals" is often translated as "evil-doers" or "malefactors." And yet, Jesus finds his place between them.

The prophet Isaiah put it this way:

> *He was numbered among the transgressors…*

Jesus is not numbered among the righteous and the religious, the bright and the beautiful, or the politically powerful and the socially connected. Jesus is numbered among the felons, the foul, and the guilty.

With little to lose, one of the criminals being crucified joined the crowd in mocking this misguided messiah. By his calculations, the one writhing in pain next to him was no kind of savior. Those "Anointed of God" don't get executed. Kings don't die with criminals. To think so was ludicrous. So, with scorn and the spit of bile, he asked, "Aren't you the Christ?"

But after a word of rebuke and caution, the second criminal pulled himself up and sputtered out a last word to Jesus:

Jesus, remember me when you come into your kingdom.

Dear friends, this is the only place in the gospels where Jesus is addressed without some other title like "Son of Man," or "Lord." I guess there's an intimacy when you're numbered among the transgressors. When you're broken and beat down, suffocating and caked in dust and excrement – all titles are gone.

It's worth noting that "remembering" in scripture is more than just recalling. To remember is more than a function of memory. This is not akin to, "Remember to pick up some milk and make an appointment for your colonoscopy." Rather, remembering in scripture often means: to act for. To remember is not just to recall but to act on behalf of…

Therefore, the criminal wasn't just asking Jesus to think of him. "Do you remember that wonderful chap I was crucified with?" No. He's asking Jesus to think of him with the power to act.

Jesus, remember me when you come into your kingdom.

It's a strange request.

Jesus certainly didn't look like he was going anywhere worth remembering. Most of his disciples had figured that out and fled. Jesus was doing his dying alone. And apparently whatever kingdom he ruled was about to come to an end. That was the purpose of execution. And yet, somehow, someway, this second criminal sees in Jesus some power to remember him.

I'm not sure that my grandmother's prayer was any different than the criminal's last words:

> *"O Lord, you saved the thief on the cross; surely you can save a sinner such as I."*

> *Jesus, remember me when you come into your kingdom.*

The plea is the same.
And Jesus responds,

> *Truly I tell you, today you will be with me in paradise.*

We often translate "paradise" here as "heaven." "Today you'll be with me in heaven." But actually, it's a rather obscure word, probably better rendered as "park" or "garden." This is the first time the word appears in scripture and it only shows up two more times. In II Corinthians Paul writes about a vision wherein he was "caught up to paradise." And in the Revelation of John, "paradise" is clearly linked to the Garden of Eden.

So, I am not sure that Jesus is talking here about a heavenly home that the criminal would be welcomed into after he expires on the cross. William Willimon puts it this way:

> *The dying thief did not begin to be with Jesus in paradise once he had drawn his last breath. The criminal began his paradise the moment he recognized the one who hung next to him in agony and humiliation on the cross was none other than his Lord, the master of his life, the sovereign of the Kingdom of God. Or, maybe he didn't know any of that about Jesus.... Because knowledge, knowing what we're doing, is far too much to expect of us,*

> *who, as Jesus said, "don't know what they're doing." All he said was, "Jesus, remember me, when you come into your kingdom." And it was enough.*

And it was enough.
Whatever paradise is, it already began there on the cross.

Truth be told, we don't know a thing about the second criminal. We don't know what crime he committed or if his family gathered at a distance to grieve his dying. We don't know if his last words were a last desperate shot or a firm statement of faith. But this faceless-nameless-criminal offers one of the most profound models of faith in scripture:

He claims his own guilt.
He names Jesus as innocent.
And he asks to be remembered.

There may be no better theology of the cross. For remember, from the vantage point of the criminal, there wasn't a resurrection. All he saw was that a dying Jesus would rule as a king. God's power is seen in Jesus dying.

Michael Gerson died recently. Gerson was the lead speech writer for President George W. Bush. A graduate of Wheaton College, after his service in the White House he worked as a columnist and political commentator. Bright, measured, conservative, Christian, Gerson was a remarkably gifted young man. He died of complications from cancer at 58.

Gerson struggled with depression for most of his adult life. In 2019 he delivered a sermon at the National Cathedral in which he wove that struggle into the proclamation of the gospel. It was a powerful word. In that sermon, he writes this:

> *But there is this difference for a Christian believer: At the end of all our striving and longing we find, not a force, but a face. All language about God is metaphorical. But the metaphor became flesh and dwelt among us.*

I love that line.

> *At the end of all our striving and longing we find, not a force, but a face.*

Dear friends, to celebrate that Christ is King is to celebrate scandal and mystery. For, we are not simply saying that an innocent Jesus died on the cross to take our guilty place and satisfy some cosmic court. Nor are we saying that the kingship of Jesus lies in an inner spiritual world and that the crucifixion was just some sort of metaphorical passion play. Neither are we saying that the cross was just the means to the end…

But we are proclaiming,
we're bearing witness to,
we're stuck with the mystery,
that the way of God is the cross.
God among us is "not a force, but a face" being crucified.
The metaphor became flesh and was crucified.
This is God's way to defeat the powers of this world.
This is God's way to kingdom and kingship.
This is God's way of being God.

Go figure.
In crucifixion there's a crown,
in powerlessness there's power,
in folly there's wisdom,
in weakness there's strength,

in suffering there's hope,
in death there's life.

I don't know what the second criminal saw in a dying Jesus. Equally befuddling is what Jesus saw in the criminal – other than his humanity.

But even with his last few words Jesus makes it clear that his kingdom is for the last, the lost, the least, the beat down, the passed over, the marginalized, and the guilty. Even as he is dying, Jesus makes it clear that his kingdom is for us.

So, this morning may we join my grandmother and
this criminal:

Remember me when you come into your kingdom.

That seems like enough.
Thanks be to God.
Amen.

God to Us

JOHN 20:1–18

Jesus has two tombs in Jerusalem.

One is inside the walls of the Old City in the Church of the Holy Sepulcher. Bells and smells, candles and frescos, and all things churchy, holy, and mysterious surround it.

The second tomb is outside of the walls of the Old City. It's a small stone sepulcher carved out of a rocky bluff, and it feels like a Bible story picture book. There are paths through flowering gardens, benches for prayer and reflection, and a gift shop for your resurrection memorabilia needs. The proprietors believe that Joseph of Arimathea owned the land and the vault. And as one priest writes, "If the Garden Tomb isn't the right place, it should be."

Two tombs. I guess it shouldn't be surprising because the gospels are surprisingly silent on the resurrection. There is scant detail of what the resurrection looked like, or sounded like, or how it happened. If you're looking for textual proof or a substantive account of the resurrection, you're looking in the wrong place. In the gospels the detail is not in the tomb but in what happens when people encounter the resurrected Lord.

Barbara Brown Taylor gets at it this way:

> *He could have stayed put, I guess, sitting there all pink and healthy between the two piles of clothes so that everyone could come in and see him, but that is not what he did. He had outgrown his tomb, which was too small a focus for the resurrection. The risen one had people to see and things to do. The living one's business was among the living.... Every time he came to his friends they became stronger, wiser, kinder, more daring. Every time he came to them, they became more like him.*
>
> *Those appearances cinch the resurrection for me, not what happened in the tomb. What happened in the tomb was entirely between Jesus and God. For the rest of us, Easter began the moment the gardener said, "Mary!" and she knew who he was. That is where the miracle happened and goes on happening – not in the tomb but in the encounter with the living Lord.*

Our text this morning features Mary's encounter with the living Lord.

There are multiple Marys in the gospels. This Mary hailed from Magdala, which historians speculate was near the north shores of the Sea of Galilee. Jesus healed her of seven demons and some believe that she was the woman of ill repute who poured perfume on the feet of Jesus, kissing and wiping his toes clean with her tears and her hair. Some traditions think she was Mary, the sister of Martha; others think there were two different Marys and two different perfume, feet, and hair incidents...

What is clear is that Mary of Magdala stuck close to Jesus. When the others abandoned him, she stayed close to the cross, and while the others slept, she got up before dawn and went to his grave.

> Even after Simon Peter and John went back, she stuck close. With the tomb empty Mary didn't go back home, contact the authorities, or go looking for him. But as the daylight pushed back the darkness, she stayed by the tomb door and wept. Maybe she was just absorbing one more brutal blow. Or maybe she just had no idea how to stay close to Jesus when she had no idea where Jesus was…

She had no idea where Jesus was until Jesus came to her.

Dear friends, the resurrection stories swing not on the disciples finding the resuscitated body of Jesus but on Jesus finding the stumped, scared, and struggling disciples. Jesus is the one who comes to them, initiates contact, and pushes back the darkness that he might be seen.

Consider…

Mary mistakes him for the gardener until he says her name.
The two walking the road to Emmaus don't recognize him until he breaks bread and disappears.
The disciples, locked in the upper room, are terrified until he appears and shows them his wounds.
Thomas doesn't believe a word of it until Jesus does the same for him.
Even his friends on the beach don't know it's him until he tells them where to catch fish.

You get the point. William Willimon puts it this way:

> *The scriptures don't report early Jesus sightings; they describe Jesus' appearances. It's an important difference. Resurrection revelation is entirely in God's hands, something God does.*

That seems like an important distinction. Whatever the resurrected Jesus was, his appearance to his followers required his initiative and his activity. That's not to dispute or deny the resurrection, but it is to suggest that what happened in the tomb doesn't seem to be a matter of attention or intention for the gospel writers.

Again, Willimon:

> *In resurrection God not only defeats death but also overcomes the limits of human perception and relationship. The first result of resurrection was not eternal life for us but rather appearance to us, revelation.*

And that is to say that God comes to us. Like sunlight pushing back the dark, God would push back our dimness and, not bound by death but loosed and alive, come to us.

God comes to us.
Maybe you've seen God.
  God comes to us in the long love of a friend.
  God comes to us in unexpected, unearned forgiveness.
  God comes to us in some sustaining support even in life's hardest losses.
  God comes to us in the life of his gathered community.
  God comes to us in the circle of an AA meeting.

God comes to us in a still, small voice.
God comes to us in acceptance for who we are.
God comes to us in the restless and relentless notion that this world was made for a Kingdom and not an empire.
God comes to us in this ancient text.
God comes to us…

The good news of Easter is not found in how Jesus, in a forgotten tomb, unwrapped the burial cloth and put on a gardener's cloak but in the living Lord who comes to us and calls us by name: Mary, Tony, Cathy, Jordon, Lori, Helen, Chris, Tom…

God comes to us and calls us by name.

Nadia Bolz-Weber writes about it this way:

> *In the incarnation, life, death, and resurrection of Christ, we see that God is for us and with that we can no longer be defined according to death, a religion-based worthiness system, or even the categories of late-stage capitalism. We are who God says we are: the forgiven, broken, and blessed children of God; the ones to whom God draws near. Nothing else gets to tell us who we are.*

One last thing…
In this wonderful tender exchange where Mary mistakes Jesus for the gardener, when she hears her name, she reaches toward him and he responds:

> *Don't hold onto me…*
> *Don't cling to me…*

The translation of the phrase is problematic. A more wooden literal translation might read, "Don't touch me…" It is a decidedly odd response. You would think even if Jesus wasn't a "hugger," in seeing her mix of astonishment, relief, and joy, he would welcome her embrace. But he says:

> *Don't hold onto me, for I have not yet ascended to the Father. Go instead…*

Maybe he means don't hold onto this body.
Or, don't hold onto this moment,
or don't try to capture the mystery of how all this happened.

Again, it's not about the resurrection; it's about the encounter with the risen Lord. Which is part of why I like the translation, "Don't cling to me…"

Don't cling, but go…
Don't cling to my body, but go and tell the others.
Don't cling, but go and bear witness to what you have seen.
Don't cling, but go and celebrate that death is defeated.
Don't cling, but go and live without fear.
Don't cling, but go…

Dear friends, scripture pays little attention to what happened in the tomb. Don't look there for certainty or clarity. But the good news of the whole sweep of scripture is encapsulated in the resurrection accounts:

God doesn't abandon us to sin, darkness, or death, but God comes to us. From the Garden of Eden to the Garden Tomb, God keeps coming to us.

And therefore, light triumphs over darkness, love over fear, forgiveness over vengeance, and goodness over evil.

Death can shake a boney fist and drive a hard bargain,
but death is not the end – resurrected life is the end.

So, don't be afraid. God comes to us.
Our confidence in the resurrection is an expression of faith.
Our comfort is not that we cling to Jesus
 but that Jesus has hold of us.
Our call is not to wait by the empty tomb
 in the early light of morn but to go.
God to us.
Us to the world.

Alleluia, Christ is risen.
Amen.

Coming Alongside

ACTS 8:26-40

Fred Rogers, of *Mr. Rogers' Neighborhood*, was invited to address the National Press Club in Washington D.C. This is a politically powerful, socially influential, and self-confident gathering. Given that they typically host leading thinkers on issues of import, some joked that with Mr. Rogers on the podium they were in for a "lite lunch."

However, when Fred Rogers began to speak, he took out a pocket watch and announced that he was going to keep two minutes of silence. Then he invited everyone in the room to think of people in their past – parents, teachers, coaches, friends – who helped make their accomplishments possible.

Mr. Rogers stood there, barely glancing at his watch, letting silence fill the room. Two minutes of silence can tick by slowly. The room was quiet, still, breathless…

But before Fred Rogers tucked away his watch, you could hear people sniffling. You could see people blinking away the mist. As people remembered those who came alongside, sacrificed, loved, and shaped them, many were moved to tears.

Tom Long tells that story and reflects on that experience:

> *If those of us who find meaning and comfort in the Christian faith were to take two minutes to reflect on how our faith came to be, few of us would say that we got it from a book, and none of us would say that we thought it up on our own. Quickly or gradually, we would begin to remember the people who spoke to us about God.... The faith we have, whether large or small, whether born of struggle or comfort, whether richly textured or barely patched together, whether grasped firmly or held onto by our fingernails, (that faith) is a part of our lives because somebody along the way had the courage and the conviction to talk to us about God and about Jesus Christ.*
>
> —From *Testimony* by Tom Long

Who came alongside you?
Who helped nurture in you a longing for God?
Who walked with you through darkness and light?
Who wrestled with you in faith and fear?
Who pointed to the mystery of God in Christ?
Who came alongside and helped shape you?

Our text is a peculiar story wherein Philip comes alongside an Ethiopian eunuch. It's one more image of the resurrection's creation-changing-reality pushing outward. It's a delightful account of the reach of God's grace in Christ.

There are three characters in this story.

Philip is either the disciple called by Jesus in the first chapter of John, or one of the seven selected to ensure equitable distribution of resources to the widows.

> Either way, the opening lines of Acts include instructions to carry the good news of the resurrection to all corners of creation. "You will be my witnesses in Jerusalem, in all of Judea and Samaria, and to the ends of the earth." And Acts 8 opens with a Philip who went "down to a city in Samaria and proclaimed the Messiah there."

Character number two: The Spirit of God shows up and directs Philip's travel plans.

> The Spirit points him toward a wilderness road, the Spirit prods him toward a chariot, the Spirit takes him away after the baptism. And the word here has the sense of being snatched up, or taken by force. The Spirit yanks Philip away, and the eunuch doesn't see him again.

Which gets us to number three: The Ethiopian eunuch.

Ethiopia serves as scriptural shorthand for the land south of Egypt; but it's also a way of suggesting the end of the world, the far reaches of creation. Being driven in a chariot, reading aloud from Isaiah, and having been to Jerusalem to worship suggests that this Ethiopian was a wealthy-well-educated-world-traveling-African-Jew. There were "God-fearers" who were Gentile converts – uncircumcised but drawn to the ethic and worship of the God of Israel. He probably falls into that category.

Our text only mentions Ethiopia once, but it names that he was a eunuch five times. Eunuchs were usually servants, castrated before puberty, and therefore deemed safe to serve among the women of a royal household. However, according to the laws in Deuteronomy they weren't to be admitted to "the assembly of the Lord."

They weren't allowed in the temple.

They were odd, outcasts, outsiders.
Their sexuality excluded them from full communion
with God and God's people.

And here is where all three characters come together. The eunuch is riding and reading when the Spirit prompts Philip to hustle up and ask if he understands what he's reading. In turn the eunuch invites him aboard. Barbara Brown Taylor likens it to a "diplomat in Washington, D.C., inviting a street preacher to join him in his late model Lexus for a little Bible study." An unlikely juxtaposition.

This is where it gets good.

The eunuch is reading in Isaiah about one who is oppressed, afflicted, shorn like a sheep, humiliated, deprived of justice, and unable to speak for his descendants. In reading he asks, "Who is this passage about? The prophet? Someone else? Me?"

He has a copy of the scripture. What he needs is someone to come alongside and help him hear the good news. So, Philip begins with that text and tells the story of God's long pursuit of *shalom* through Jesus Christ. He tells of a Messiah who would not be a conquering king but a suffering servant. He tells of a kingdom where all are welcome…

Dear friends, it seems entirely plausible that this eunuch, having been to Jerusalem and heading back to Ethiopia, is wondering if there is a place for him.

Was his ethnicity or his sexuality a barrier?
Was he included or excluded?
Was he welcomed or cast out?
Was he accepted or was he condemned?

His sexuality was assigned him. His otherness was not a matter of will or weakness. He was simply who he was. But who among us gets to choose our ethnicity, gender, orientation, genetic material, or family of origin? Who among us gets to choose?

I hope the Spirit led Philip to turn a few chapters forward in Isaiah, for there is a beautiful passage where the captives, the poor, the sick, the outcasts are welcomed, and the house of God is called "a house of prayer for all nations." Listen to just a few lines:

> *This is what the Lord says: To the eunuchs who keep my Sabbaths, who choose what pleases me and hold fast to my covenant – to them I will give within my temple and its walls a memorial and a name better than sons and daughters; I will give them an everlasting name that will endure forever.*

On a stretch of road in the middle of nowhere, Philip comes alongside this eunuch to tell him that he belongs to God in Christ…

He is loved and accepted exactly as he is.
He is welcomed within the household of God.
He is a child of God.
The resurrection ripples out past Hebrews and Hellenists to an exotic Ethiopian eunuch. Thanks be to God!

Does that read too much into this story?

Deb was a dear friend in college and a gifted singer-songwriter. Her voice was clear, effortless, and human. There was nothing pretentious or showy. She loved Jesus, loved college, and loved life. The college couldn't have been prouder.

> She was sent out to be the face and voice of the institution. From coast to coast, she was sent to churches, to meet parents, to connect with alumni, and to recruit new students. She was our very own Amy Grant.

A couple years after graduation, while working for the college, after years of praying and pleading, after years of turmoil, Deb told the truth. She went to the trusted college chaplain and said, "I'm a lesbian. For as long as I've known myself, I've known that I was uniquely and wonderfully made. I need to tell the truth about who I am."

> He responded that she needed to resign immediately, or repent, change, and tell the college president. He gave her 24 hours or he would go to the administration. She opted for conversion therapy – and little by little lost more of herself. Beat down by depression, she eventually left the college.

As Deb came out friends shunned her, argued with her, and bludgeoned her with the Bible – that she knew and loved. They promised that they would pray for her healing. Guys thought that she just needed the right guy. Girls wondered about the nature of their relationship. She was fully alive in her own skin and her heart was broken.

I wonder what would have happened if someone else would have come alongside, opened up scripture, and said, "You belong to God in Christ. You are loved and accepted exactly as you are. You are welcome within the household of God. You are a child of God. The resurrection ripples out to you. Thanks be to God."

Dear friends, I am not trying to stir up trouble. The trouble is in the text. I am trying to point out that Acts seems to insist that no one is excluded from God's welcome.

One more thing…
As the Spirit, and Philip, and the eunuch traveled that dusty-desert-highway, they came upon some water and the eunuch asked,

> *Look, here is some water. What can stand in the way of my being baptized?*

There were plenty of barriers. The eunuch "belonged to the wrong nation, worked for the wrong sovereign, and possessed the wrong sexuality." But listen to how Tom Long describes what happens next:

> *"What is to prevent me from being baptized?" asked the eunuch.*
>
> *"Absolutely nothing," whispered the Spirit. "Absolutely nothing."*
>
> *So, the eunuch commanded the chariot to stop, and he was baptized right on the spot. Walls of prejudice and prohibition that had stood for generations came tumbling down, blown down by the breath of God's Holy Spirit, and another man who felt lost and humiliated was found and restored by the wideness of God's grace.*
>
> —From *Feasting on the Word* by Tom Long

Thanks be to God.
May it be so for all people.

And even as Christ has come alongside us,
may we come alongside others.
Amen.

Note: *A good portion of this – flow, organization, and content – came from Tom Long.*

Burrowed into the Bowels

ROMANS 8:18–24

As the spring sun loosened winter's grip, I was on a morning ride with other bicycle racers. Four men with shaved legs, dressed in colorful cycling apparel, rolling along in a 23-mile-an-hour pace line. It was a motion of grace; creation was in a full-voiced chorus of joy.

I took my turn at the front of the line and then drifted to the back – smooth and silent, the wedding of body and machine and team. Suddenly I caught a glimpse of a ball of fur on the shoulder of the road. Even more suddenly that ball of fur shot between my front tire and my back tire. With a little bump I rolled over that fast flurry of fur…

What was that?

As my friends rolled on unaware, I glanced over my shoulder, and there, flopping on the pavement, was a squirrel. Squashed. He lurched and staggered about the road. Nobody else saw it. I didn't know what to do.

And in that split second, as we were sailing up the road, I thought, "What's wrong with this picture?" In the corner of a *shalom*-morning there was a smashed squirrel. On an overwhelmingly good morning one of God's little creatures met his demise under the wheels of an Italian racing bike.

As a high school teacher, I recounted that ridiculous story because it made kids laugh, and it opened all sorts of questions:

Is Lycra ever acceptable attire for a teacher?
Was death part of God's original intention for creation?
Does God have a grand plan?
Is there any sense or sovereignty in the sufferings of this world?

It's a trite story, but it pushed open the door for discussion. Kids knew the goodness of creation. They told stories of catching a glimpse of God's hand delightfully traced in the created order, but they also knew that something was wrong with this picture.

They knew that things were foul and fatally flawed.
They were the children of 9/11 and school shootings.
They were on the backside of Hiroshima and the Holocaust.
They knew that under the sheen something was sick-unto-death.
They knew that creation is broken.

To quote Neil Plantinga:

> *Creation speaks out of both sides of its mouth. It still sings and rings, but it also groans. As Paul says, "the whole creation has been groaning" for release from its "bondage to decay."*

The language that scripture attaches to this state of affairs is "sin."

It's not just a matter of ignorance or a few bad apples.

It's not just a moral scale that is slightly out of kilter.
It's not just the cumulative consequences of bad choices.
It's sin…

I was trying to get high school students to expand their understanding of sin. For many of them, sin was little more than adolescent indiscretions – their naughty thoughts, their lusts and longings, their pint-sized peccadilloes. But scripture offers that sin is more than the sum of its parts. That creation itself is bent, bound, broken, and born into a state of being from which it can't extricate itself.

There is something else,
some spirit,
some curse,
some enslavement in the very stuff of creation.

Many of you know that on a beautiful spring morning my father was murdered a few feet away from me and my family. I guess the "sin" was the murder – the blatant disregard for the sanctity of life that caused Clarence Hayes, with no provocation, to pull the trigger. Guilty.

But, on that Sunday morning, in that church parking lot, I also remember thinking that this was just one thread in an intractable knot of poverty, addiction, inadequate health care, a culture of violence, easy access to guns, unemployment, mass incarceration, racism, limited educational opportunities, mental illness, crack cocaine, national indifference, etc., etc., etc. It was all a knotted mess that choked off *shalom* and fouled God's intention for creation. The murder was more than just one expression of sin for which the murderer was culpable – it also seemed like something evil was "burrowed into the bowels" (Plantinga) of creation.

Again, Neil Plantinga is helpful here:

> *Evil is what's wrong with the world, and it includes trouble in nature as well as in human nature. It includes disease as well as theft, birth defects as well as character defects. We might define evil as any spoiling of shalom, any deviation from the way God wants things to be. Thinking along those lines we can see that sin is a subset of evil; it's a member of a group. All sin is evil, but not all evil is sin.*

Our text this morning proclaims that sin is more than just the work of humanity – no mattered how depraved. Rather, there is something in the fabric and fiber of the cosmos that is corrupted and in bondage. And not of its own choice. The ground under our feet is so vandalized of the *shalom* that God intended that it too is groaning for healing and release.

Calvin uses the language that:

> *There is no fragment or particle of the world, which, in the grip of the knowledge of its present misery, does not hope for resurrection.*

And I would offer that the corruption of creation finds expression in institutions, systems, diseases, economics, environment, sexuality, and spirituality, and…
And it can't all be tied directly to the will, missteps, or activity of humanity.

That doesn't mean there's no goodness and mercy in this world, but it does mean that there are forces unto death that are bigger than we are. And, therefore, no education, no enlightenment, no religion, no rationality, no purchase, no pill, no progress, no therapy will be able to fully restore *shalom*,

or turn the tide,

or liberate the earth,

or salvage creation.

I offer that not as an excuse for inaction,

or to massage our guilt,

or to ignore this world and wait for another,

or to shrug off earth-keeping, justice-seeking, and peace-building as nothing more than putting bandages on a terminal patient.

I think the goodness of creation and the image of God that is in all people calls forth our very best in seeking *shalom* and using whatever gifts we have for the good of others. But I also know that there is something in creation that we can't overcome. There is something that is beyond our capacity to save, rescue, fix, heal.

The Belgic Confession puts it this way:

> *It is the corruption of all nature – an inherited depravity which even infects small infants in their mother's womb, and the root which produces in man every sort of sin. It is therefore so vile and enormous in God's sight that it is enough to condemn the human race, and it is not abolished or wholly uprooted even by baptism, seeing that sin constantly boils forth as though from a contaminated spring.*

Dear friends, for a whole host of friends that I love, all this talk about sin and an evil that is manifest in creation is an antiquated-bowl-full-of-religious-balderdash. It sounds as plausible as Muggles in Middle Earth – to mix fantasies. And I know that my thinking here is sloppy and not fully developed or articulated…

> Does it mean that evil is in the very cellular structure of creation?
> And if evil isn't in the stuff of creation, then where is it?
> What is it?
> Does evil have personhood or a power outside of God?
> If so, where did it come from?
> And, why wouldn't God, who purportedly created and loves this world, do something immediately to end the suffering and sorrow that defines so much of this world?

You get the idea. And, as one who often has a front row seat to the human condition, I have no answers for why that which is evil and cruel often seems to win the day. But, given the daily record, given any honest reading of history, given that "the line between good and evil cuts through the heart of every human being," I don't have any other way to frame the human condition…

> It's hard to write it all off to ignorance, or an inadequate rationality, or the slow pace of progress. There is something at work in creation that's beyond our ability to change that ultimately leads to death.

Sin.
Evil.
Death.

Therefore, we join creation in groaning for healing, in groaning for salvation, in groaning for life. We long for something more than the snatching of sinners' souls from Satan's grasp. But we join creation in groaning for the healing of

every hunger,
every hatred,
every lost species,
every depleted resource,
every malignancy,
every loss,
every square inch,
and every broken heart.

May the very ground under our feet be restored to the *shalom* that God intends.

Amen.

Reframing Creation

II CORINTHIANS 5:16–21

I saw a doctor about the recovery process from my car-versus-bicycle crash and was taken aback when she said, "It looks like you've really embraced acceptance."

I thought, you have no idea about my internal landscape and how far away I am from acceptance…

When I recounted that conversation with a therapist/friend he said, "Acceptance is an emotionally charged word and not very helpful. Rather than acceptance think of adaptation. A measure of health is how we adapt to change."

That little one-word-shift, from accept to adapt, has made a big difference. Rather than struggling with acceptance, I now think about how best to adapt to these challenges. Changing how I frame these ongoing issues has helped change how I approach recovery.

As it turns out, there's a method in therapy called "reframing." The therapist doesn't provide answers or offer techniques, but they ask questions in such a way that the frame changes. Like from accept to adapt. The picture doesn't change; the frame changes.

Think of it this way: the meaning that any life-event has for us depends upon the frame in which we perceive it. So, if we can change the frame, the meaning changes; and if the meaning changes, our responses or behaviors can also change.

Reframing is probably
more art than technique,
more grace than law,
more imagination than skill,
but as the frame is changed,
we see the picture differently.

Paul writes to the church in Corinth that because of Christ, creation has been reframed. As the frame changes, the meaning changes, and our responses or behaviors change.

Consider…
Part of Paul's story is a dramatic conversion. He was bowled over and blinded by the light on the road to Damascus. Metaphorically speaking, when his vision was restored, he saw things differently.

He saw Jesus, who he'd been persecuting, in a new frame.
He saw the relationship between God and humanity in a new frame.

Listen again to Paul:

So, from now on we regard no one from
a worldly point of view.
Though we once regarded Christ this way,
we do so no longer.

In Greek it reads that we regarded Jesus and one another "according to the flesh," or from a "fleshy" point of view. In other words, Paul once regarded Jesus as no more and no less than any other flesh-and-blood human being wandering this planet. But then Paul encountered Jesus, and he had to reframe everything.

From now on we regard no one according to the flesh…

Paul sets up a sort of parallel between seeing Jesus differently and seeing everyone else differently. He's not suggesting that we see one another as divine (like Jesus), but there's
a new perspective, a new point of view, a new frame.

Therefore, dear friends, what's the outline of this new frame?
What's this new point of view?
What if we came at it this way?

We're all broken.
We all have issues.
We're all fleshy and flawed.
We're all dead in sin.
And yet, we're reconciled to God through Christ.
We're made right with God through the life, death, and resurrection of Jesus.
That's a done deal.

Paul puts it this way, literally:

Therefore, if anyone is in Christ – new creation!
The old things have passed away, the new has come into being.

Thanks be to God.

The question here is…

Is Paul writing about individuals as new creations, or is he referring to something bigger, broader, more inclusive, and more cosmic? Something that requires a new frame? Are only individuals who are "in Christ" a new thing, or is creation itself somehow changed?

Traditionally we've been given a frame that sees people in different categories. We see some as lost, damned, prodigals, and the fleshy enemies of God. But, as the frame changes, how we view the picture changes.

So, in Christ there's a new creation, a new frame. Therefore, rather than seeing others from a worldly point of view, what if we saw others as belonging to God in Christ? What if we saw others as reconciled to God in Christ? They may not know it. They may not recognize it. They may deny it, fight it, ignore it, besmirch it, and be too cool for it, but that doesn't change the reality.

So, from now on we regard no one from
a worldly point of view.
Though we once regarded Christ this way,
we do so no longer.

What would it mean if we saw friends, neighbors, and enemies not as objects of mission, targets for conversion, or simply not one of us, but we changed the frame and saw them as we are: broken and loved by God in Christ? Would that change how we love, serve, welcome, and walk with friend, neighbor, and enemy?

I know this makes us nervous...

Here he goes again – all fuzzy on hell. Clearly some of us are new creations and others are old creations. We live in a world that's rent asunder by evil. Clearly not all people belong to God in Christ. The Reformed tradition has long held that Jesus died only for those whom Jesus chose. We like those categories. You can't muddle that up with talk of a new creation. We're happy with the old frame.

But Doug Bratt writes about it this way:

> *God didn't let people kill Jesus before raising him from the dead just to offer people some kind of religious deal. In Christ God creates something "new." God's work in Christ changes the world. God transforms history, making all things new. Those "things" include not just the whole creation and its creatures, but also Christians' attitudes toward our neighbors. God doesn't just long to be reconciled to people who declare ourselves to be God's enemies. God also longs for people who view our neighbors as our enemies to be reconciled to each other.*

I mentioned a few weeks ago that recent changes in the American church have been referred to as the "great sorting." We're retreating into political/cultural silos. If we're still going to church, we're finding our way to congregations that affirm and encourage our self-interests. We're sorting out...

Maybe that's all we can do. We're weary of pandemic politics, denominational discord, covid controversies, and issues of sexuality or race or whatever current-culture-war-trope is being trotted out. At least in church we should be with our own tribe...

But! And this is a big but…

But Paul proclaims that we should regard ***no one*** from a worldly point of view. Because in Christ there's a new creation where love trumps fear, forgiveness supplants judgment, reconciliation is the will and work of God, and death no longer has the last word.

And this new creation doesn't hang in the balance. Today we may only catch a whiff, only see a spark, and only hear a whisper, but ultimately this new creation will overwhelm and fill up every square inch.

And we're emissaries of that reality, ambassadors of that reconciliation. So, don't look at yourself or at others in an old frame, but reframe as a new creation…

And, dear friends, that would mean church communities that are not reflections of tribalism, political hubris, or theological certitude but that are full of broken people, who belong to God in Christ, simply trying to welcome, love, listen, and bear witness to this new creation.

We long for churches that are busy building new frames in keeping with a new creation. N.T. Wright summarizes it like this:

> *Made for spirituality, we wallow in introspection. Made for joy, we settle for pleasure. Made for justice, we clamor for vengeance. Made for relationship, we insist on our own way. Made for beauty, we are satisfied with sentiment. But new creation has already begun. The sun has begun to rise. Christians are called to leave behind, in the tomb of Jesus Christ, all that belongs to the brokenness and incompleteness of the present world. It is time, in the power of the Spirit, to take up our proper role, our fully*

human role, as agents, heralds, and stewards of the new day that is dawning. That, quite simply, is what it means to be a Christian: to follow Jesus Christ in the new world, God's new world, which he has thrown open before us.

Thanks be to God.

In one frame, these are just cubes of Wonder Bread and shot glasses of Welch's Grape Juice in service of a religious ritual with little drama or expectation.

But reframed, this is a foretaste of a new creation. Reframed, this is an appetizer for a banquet thrown for one who was lost but now is found, was dead but now is alive. Reframed, this a sign and seal of the feast of a coming Kingdom. Reframed, this is a table set for the last, the lost, and the least…

So, come to the table, where all are called and all are welcomed.
For God in Christ is doing a new thing.
Thanks be to God.

Amen.

What Would You Say?

I TIMOTHY 1:12–17

The hospital parking lot was almost empty – visiting hours were hours away. The only cars in the lot were for emergencies or family members that had spent the night curled up in chairs and pacing the hospital halls. I pulled into a spot in the sun, gulped down my breakfast iced-tea, and walked slowly into the hospital.

There was no need to hurry. They didn't expect Edna to make it through the day. I knew I would find the family gathered around the bed, or in the waiting room wondering how to wait for a loved one to die. I didn't know what to say, or what to read, or what to pray. There was no need to hurry.

Edna was in her late fifties, a divorced mother of two. If life had dealt her a bad hand, she'd crumpled the cards. Whatever hope or joy there may have once been seemed buried by drinking too much, eating too much, and stewing too much. Whatever color there was to her cheek was a smudge of rose-red-rouge. Her voice was thick with smoke and phlegm and anger. She was mad most of the time.

Mad at her kids for not calling,
mad at her ex-husband for walking away,
mad at her boss for brushing her off,

mad at God for not making things better,
mad at the Mexicans and Muslims and the "coloreds,"
mad at the catalogues she got in the mail full of stuff that
she couldn't fit or couldn't afford,
mad at herself…

Her job clerking at an insurance office paid the bills, but there was no margin for error or extravagance. She really wanted to help her daughter with her new baby and help her son fix up his truck. She dreamed of taking one of those cruises in the Caribbean to drink Mai-Tais on the beach and maybe feel alive in her own skin.

The hospital receptionist asked my relationship to the patient. I told her, "Pastor." She looked at me skeptically. In the elevator I asked God to help me be present and helpful in some way. I didn't know what you pray for.

"Dear Lord, help Edna die peacefully and quickly…"

"Dear God, bring her back to life…"

The family encircled the bed. Her daughter was holding her hand. Her son was sitting in a chair with his head in his hands. Her sister and brother-in-law were standing at the end of the bed. They seemed relieved to see me, mostly because I was just a familiar face in the midst of strangers.

Two days earlier no one expected to be here, but after a series of strokes, and a heart without a lot of fight, and a history of poor health…

The doctors said there wasn't much they could do. It had to do with where the strokes were located. They could manage the pain, but her systems were shutting down. It could be a matter of hours or a matter of days. There was no way of knowing. We were waiting for her to die.

We talked.
We held hands around the bed and prayed.
We told stories about Edna.
We sat in silence.
We offered coffee.
We all wanted to help somehow.
We talked about the weather.

Suddenly Edna's son picked up his head and asked if we could go for a walk. We were barely out of the ICU when, before I could whisper one word, he looked up again, wincing to hold back tears, his lips trembling, and said, "Do you think she'll go to hell?"

"I… I… I don'…"

He didn't wait. He said, "I think she will. Big deal, she went to church. She's been killing herself for years. She didn't take care of herself; she didn't take her medicine; she didn't do what the doctor said. All she did was watch television and smoke. It's like she wanted to die. It's like, it's like she committed suicide. And God doesn't forgive that…"

He turned away with his whole face twitching.

In the silence of a hospital hallway, what do you say about God?
What do you say to a young man wondering about his mother?
What do you say about the nature of God?
What would you say?

Paul says to Timothy, that even though he had been a bad-bad man,

even though he had been a blasphemer and a persecutor,
even though he was (depending on your translation) dramatically arrogant or a violent man,
even though he had been the coat-check-boy for those who stoned Stephen,
even though he "laid waste to the church, entering house after house, dragging off men and women and putting them in prison,"
even though he was the "worst of sinners,"
God had shown him mercy.

In describing himself, Paul stacks up the terms of an insolent, raging, ruthless, unforgivable existence, and then in stark, startling contrast says literally:

Mercy was had on me...

Mercy was had on me...

There's a passive quality to the sentence structure.
Mercy wasn't something that he earned or that he grasped.
Mercy wasn't something that he deserved or that he did.
Mercy wasn't something that he managed or mustered.
Mercy wasn't something that he believed.
Mercy was done unto him.

Mercy was had on me...

The word for mercy here has the sense of extending help to those in misery. Not just as a matter of legal transaction, or economic exchange, or as the outcome of a system, but there is some manner of tender affection,

some lovingkindness,

some commiserating,
some motion of the heart.
Mercy comes from the heart of God.

So, Paul writes to Timothy, his "true son in the faith," that God is merciful.

What would you say in a hospital hallway?

In the summer of 1521, Philipp Melanchthon wrote to his good friend Martin Luther asking him how to answer the charge that those who would reform the church neglected pilgrimages, fasts, and other traditional forms of piety. Melanchthon was asking Luther if there wasn't something that we had to do in order to hold up our end of the bargain.

Luther wrote back:

> *If you are a preacher of mercy, do not preach an imaginary but the true mercy. If the mercy is true, you must therefore bear the true, not an imaginary sin. God does not save those who are only imaginary sinners. Be a sinner, and let your sins be strong, but let your trust in Christ be stronger, and rejoice in Christ who is the victor over sin, death, and the world...*

What would you say in a hospital hallway?

Join Paul, and Luther, and say that our only hope is in the mercy of God expressed in Christ Jesus.

For, if there is some ledger that we have to balance,
if there is some acceptable standard for piety,
if there is some measure that we have to meet,

if it comes down to what we do – then we're all screwed.
But if it is a matter of mercy – then thanks be to God
in Christ Jesus!

My young friend in the hospital hallway was weighing life on the scales of "deserve." Even in his grief and anger there was a standard of right behavior that had to be met in order to meet God, and he wondered if his mother matched up. In that framework, good works, good people, and good behavior get rewarded – and flaws, failings, and fallenness gets punished.

But Paul, Martin Luther, and maybe you know that when our backs are against the wall, all we really have to offer is our sin – and not our imaginary sin.

Dear friends, you may not have a dramatic story of conversion on the way to Damascus or Detroit, and you may not be the "worst of sinners," but if there is any saving that needs to be done

it won't swing on the scales of "deserve,"
it won't be a matter of just desserts,
it won't be because we get what's coming to us…
It will be because *Christ Jesus came into the world*
to save sinners.
It will be because *mercy was had on us.*

Maybe it's helpful to think about it this way…
Mountain climbers set up a base camp from which they make their attempt to reach the mountain summit. Base camp is where they start their ascent, and it's the place to which they return if they have trouble. It's their home for the journey.

I would offer that our base camp is staked in God's mercy. Even as we would be disciples of Jesus, even as we would be students, followers, or apprentices of Jesus, our camp is in his mercy.

The life of faith isn't a way to do the right thing, and follow the right path, and somehow be good enough to meet God's demands. Rather, faith is the journey that stumbles, dances, or climbs out of mercy. And faith is a journey that will always go home to mercy.

And in the hallway of a hospital…
mercy is our only hope,
our only confidence,
and our only comfort.

What else would you say?

Christ Jesus came into the world to save sinners.

Thanks be to God.
Amen.

Back to Basics

PHILIPPIANS 2:1–11

I'm told that after being hit by a car I repeatedly asked the doctor, "When will I be able to run?" I had a severed artery, a fractured femur, a blown-out knee, a separated pelvis, a gaping hole in my leg, a rack of broken ribs, a punctured lung, was severely concussed, seeing double, and I was asking about running…

I don't remember the first week in the hospital, but I do remember trying to move as soon as they'd let me. I remember trying to walk without the walker, or the brace, or the boot. I remember trying to get across the room, to the end of the hall, to the end of the block, and eventually trying to run at night on empty streets. I wanted to get back to the only life I knew, so as soon as I could muster any movement, I was on a bike, in the pool, or on the road. I was trying to get back to basics.

Pandemic policies, the denomination's human sexuality debate, the splintering of the American body-politic, the soup of information and misinformation, the ebb and flow of people retiring, graduating, taking new jobs and moving, and funerals for friends and family, and, and, and… And it can feel like Hope Church got hit by a car.

Dear friends, there's no missing that these last years have taken a toll. We did the best we could to navigate the road in front of us, but if you measure things like worship attendance, numbers of kids in programs, babies, baptisms, and transfers – it feels like we got knocked into a ditch.

The only measure that matters is: How does a church proclaim and embody the gospel? How does it gather and nurture followers of Jesus Christ?

> But over the last few years it's been easy to look at other measures and get discouraged, or think we should try something different, or do something different, or be something different. It's been easy to wonder if we should change to thrive or just to survive.

But in discouragement, I look back to basics.

> The only movement I can muster is toward the basic commitments of the only life we've known. And for Hope, getting back to basics means trying to follow our text as a way to live out the gospel. In that spirit, let us consider the basics of Hope Church.

The beginning of our text is addressed to a community:

> *If you* (plural) *have any encouragement from being united with Christ, if any comfort from his love, if any common sharing in the Spirit, if any tenderness and compassion...*

then it will be found in life together.

Paul writes to the *ekklesia* in Philippi. *Ekklesia* is the Greek word for church, it literally means "the called-out ones." The church is called out to be an alternative community – a community united in identification with Jesus Christ.

At our most basic we are called together – not by ethnicity, education, political persuasion, worship style, economic class, sexual orientation, or theological impulse but by belonging to Jesus Christ.

> You may have better friends in other places, you may be more comfortable with others, you may have disagreements with one another, but at its best Hope Church is an intergenerational-web of mutually-dependent people who are united in Christ and value others above themselves.

Community is hard to do.

> We live 45 minutes in all directions. New people wonder how they'll find substantive connections; old people harbor old habits. We've all got busy lives, boatloads of issues, and I can bear witness that political posturing on social media doesn't serve us well. There's hurt, disappointment, and bewilderment on both sides of the aisle. But to embody the gospel is to be in community. Against the tide of individualism, loneliness, and tribalism, we're longing for, searching after, and trying to build community – united in Christ.

Our text reads that our *relationships with one another* would arise out of the same *attitude of mind*. That's an odd phrase because the translator is trying to communicate that *mind* here means more than thinking or rationality. It's the fullness of human disposition, psyche, worldview, and a way of relating to creation. And therefore, to follow Christ is not just to be part of a community, but it invites a habit of heart and mind.

This morning we're starting a new year of Sunday school and adult education. We've launched new seasons of *God Loves Me* and *Children in Worship*, and we'll soon start a new worship education class for kids and a Bible study for women. I hope other studies will start because even with all of its complexity and obscurity, we find our bearings in this ancient text and in the life, death, and resurrection of Jesus.

> And living in a post-biblical culture, that calls for a measure of biblical literacy and the deep roots of the Reformed tradition. Contemporary culture has a curriculum that shapes mind, body, and spirit; the *ekklesia* is called to a different curriculum and that requires an investment of time, attention, and self. A once-a-week-17-minute-sermon isn't going to cut it.

Community.
Education.

The second half of our text is thought to be one of the first Christian hymns. Therefore, it's helpful to think of the first verses of our text as a preacher encouraging a congregation and building to a homiletical high point.

> *In humility value others above yourselves, not looking to your own interests, but each to the interests of others. In your relationships with one another have the same attitude of mind Christ Jesus had, who…*

And then just at that crescendo the preacher breaks into song.

> *Who, being in very nature God, did not consider equality with God something to be used to his advantage; rather he made himself nothing…*

And out rolls this beautiful hymn about the movement from deity to death. The Greek word here is *kenosis* – emptying. This early hymn proclaims the staggering mystery of a self-emptying God.

That's to say that we're little more than a liturgical-country-club or a pencil-necked-book-club if our life together is just community and education. To be shaped in the mind of Christ is to be engaged in this world in love and service.

> We exist for *kenosis* – to empty ourselves for the sake of others. That's hard to define and even harder to live into, but by vocation and avocation, we're called to pursue, bear witness to, and empty ourselves for the sake of creation's *shalom*.

In a couple weeks Moises and Erin Pacheco will mark one year in their own worship space – as they plant Grace in Garfield Park. They can testify that it's harder than they thought, but with Hope's blessing and support they're living into their calling to birth a new multi-ethnic-intergenerational-church.

> We've got folks serving breakfast this morning at Roseland Christian Ministries. We provide lunches every month, have folks helping every week, and that little southside congregation knows us as partners. We recently helped sponsor and settle an Afghan refugee family. We're consistently linked up in support of Elim, Together We Cope, and Christian schools in all sorts of contexts. Our deacons list opportunities for service almost every week, and they're looking at new missionary support in the future. And on and on and on…
>
> > And in twenty years we've only once missed paying 100% of our Denominational Ministry Shares. Almost

> one-third of our annual budget goes out from Hope for work and witness all over the world. Thanks be to God.

Community.
Education.
Servanthood.
Back to the basics.

Peter Marty – pastor of a big Lutheran church and editor of *The Christian Century* – called this week. By upbringing and career there are few better equipped to talk about the church in America. He told me that when they got the post-pandemic-all-clear they cancelled their worship livestream. They kept a sermon podcast, but they turned off the cameras. He said,

> *What we do in worship requires our bodies, holy and broken. Singing together, celebrating the eucharist, seeing one another, listening, praying – it's too abundant to leave to a flat screen. It means too much, and in our traditions, it just makes for bad TV.*

He's right…
We're not going to turn off our cameras (just yet); our livestream has been helpful for folks in all sorts of spaces and places, but to get back to basics is to be gathered in worship.

Our text descends to death on a cross and from there it reaches to the highest place in heaven wherein all people – in time and space – fall on their knees to worship Jesus Christ. The movement is from *kenosis* to cosmic lordship. Our text starts in being united in Christ, traverses through the cross, and ends in all creation joined in worship.

Worship is the one constant that gathers us together.
We're united in bowing and confessing that Jesus Christ is Lord.

Not unlike coffee or cabernet, worship at Hope is an acquired taste. Our liturgical-folksy-worship and quirky-preaching takes some getting used to. We're consistently led by intergenerational voices in prayer, liturgy, and music. We invest in the gifts of Dora, Lynn, Dave, Bev, and Erin because each brings a unique musical voice, draws out the gifts of others, and is committed to congregational singing. There's no worship-tainment. There's a reason they're in the back of the sanctuary…

Community.
Education.
Servanthood.
Worship.

To do less than that is to forsake our reason for being.
To do more than that is to lose track of our reason for being.

Paul's word to the Philippians has been our basic framework for nineteen years.

I don't know where the road will lead.
I don't know the coming splits, bumps, rocky passages,
and slippery slopes.
I can't see the next crash.
But no matter the road, we're called back to these basics.
May God continue to bless our life together.

Amen.

A Tale of Two Cities

REVELATION 21:1–6

It was the best of times, it was the worst of times,
it was the age of wisdom, it was the age of foolishness,
it was the epoch of belief, it was the epoch of incredulity,
it was the season of Light, it was the season of Darkness,
it was the spring of hope, it was the winter of despair,
we had everything before us, we had nothing before us,
we were all going direct to Heaven, we were all going
direct the other way – in short…

In short, it was college and I was twenty. I was a wide-eyed lad freshly landed in the big city for the "Chicago Metropolitan Semester." And one night with cute co-eds from Hope and guys from Calvin, all full of themselves, we made our way to the 95th floor of the John Hancock building. There's a bar up there with nothing but small tables and big windows. The city was laid out at our feet. As far as we could see:

well-ordered lights,
architectural gems,
the silent motion of cars,
the darkness of the lake,
the ribbons of rivers weaving through this city
rising up out of the plains.

It was the best of times, and through smoked glass – attractive, dynamic, intoxicating, mysterious – I was falling in love with Chicago. While others talked and laughed, I dreamt about life in the city.

> Maybe I would live in a loft with great woodwork in a neighborhood that had cool watering holes, quaint restaurants, lively conversation, vibrant music, a bounty of bookstores, and a delightful diversity of people. Maybe I'd live where Grace and ivy converge. My life would look like the love child of Patagonia and Restoration Hardware. I dreamt of being urban; there would be no sub-urban life for me.

The city is a collision of the powerful and the poor, crass commercialism and the finest of art and architecture, the politics of race and the spice of ethnic communities, the crushing gears of urban systems and the dignity of daily work. Spirit and cement, Christ and culture…

> At that moment it was all in front of me,
> and around me,
> and overwhelming me,
> and romancing me,
> from 95 stories up.

Later that night we paid the hefty tab, parted company, and headed for our apartments. My friends headed north, and I headed south. I was alone hopping the El, changing buses, and walking. I slipped into the embrace of my new love.

> Only now there were bars on every window and chains on every door. Every corner was a liquor store or a storefront church. Vacant lots and abandoned buildings tarnished the shining city. The issues of race and violence and poverty were crushing and complex and laced with fear.

I was in the bosom of the city that looked so good from 95 stories up. Only now she seemed loud, dirty, broken, and stinky. Now she felt cold, confusing, chaotic, and I didn't matter to her at all. I felt like a junior high kid with a crush on a teacher. I felt like a foolish kid from Iowa.

It was the best of times, it was the worst of times...

Adam raised Cain. And Cain – who murdered his brother Abel – is noted as the first city builder in Scripture. In Genesis 11 we read this account of city building:

> *Then they said, "Come, let us build for ourselves a city, with a tower that reaches to the heavens, so that we may make a name for ourselves, and not be scattered over the face of the whole earth."*

Babel is the first skyscraper, but the first city that has any prominence in scripture is Babylon. From Genesis to Revelation, Babylon rears her head as a symbol for the city of man – to borrow language from Saint Augustine.

Babylon represents the best of what we are
and what we can build.
Babylon represents the center of human activity.
Babylon represents the high pinnacle of human endeavor.
Maybe Babylon represents all that I fell in love with...

And yet throughout the biblical narrative, Babylon is seen as a harlot. She calls. She lures. She entices. She promises. Her beauty can be a dizzying whirl of hope and expectation, but if you scrape off the makeup and see past the façade, if the towers come tumbling down, you will find a whore – broken, loud, vapid, narcissistic, cheap, and chaotic.

And you and I don't matter to her at all.
Babylon, the city of man.

But there's another city.
There's another city in scripture.
There's another city that I've seen.

Years ago, I came to Chicago with a group of east-coast-high-school-kids for a week of service with a group of south-side-high-school-kids. The plan was that they would work together planting gardens and rehabbing homes. But it rained hard and steady every day. There was little that we could do, and we weren't sure what to do. Until we decided to throw a dinner party…

So, Ivy League kids and Chicago Public School kids made the invitations together, planned the menu together, shopped for the food together, decorated the church together, fixed the meal together, and threw a party together.

That evening the church filled up with people: street walkers and students, crack addicts and children from around the corner who hadn't changed their clothes all week, gay men and straight women, school teachers and the mentally ill, ex-cons and future cons, kids with bright eyes, men with dull eyes from too many years on the street, and one blind grandmother. The church filled up with God's people.

The kids proudly filled up the plates of all who came to the table with hot dogs, macaroni and cheese, curly fries, and brownies. The laughter was free, the party was loud, and the dinner conversations bridged the gaps of age, gender, race, and education. Children scurried around the tables and jumped

Double Dutch. Homeless men filled their pockets with left-overs. No one went home hungry of stomach or hungry of soul.

At one point we held hands in a circle and together we sang the "black doxology." Same lyrics, different tune. The kids from the east didn't know either, the kids from the southside taught them. Together they raised their voices in song. And I caught a glimpse of a different city.

I know in the big picture this meal was only a small pixel. In the big city it was no big deal. It didn't alter public policy or change the economic landscape. It was a fleeting moment that would be quickly forgotten. It was a veneer of makeup over a harsh human face. It was nothing bigger than a mustard seed.

But I caught a glimpse of the new city, the new Jerusalem,
the city of God.
And at least symbolically, at least briefly,
tears were brushed away
and there was no death or mourning or crying or pain,
and the dwelling of God was with people,
and in the belly of the harlot,
we had a banquet for the bride.

Babylon and New Jerusalem serve as bookends to scripture. They are the symbolic poles that hold the tension of the biblical narrative and frame the unfolding story of creation's redemption. They capture the movement of history from brokenness to healing, from confusion to clarity, from chaos to consummation; or to borrow the language of Handel's Hallelujah Chorus,

The kingdom of this world; is become the kingdom of our Lord and of his Christ.

Dear friends, you and I are wedged in the middle. We live in the tension. Our journey is traversed between the city of man and the city of God.

That's not to say that we have dual citizenship in two different cities.
That's not to say that we live in two different realities simultaneously.
That's not to say that we skip between two different worlds.
Rather, that is to say that this world is moving toward its restoration, renewal, reclamation, and redemption…

It is a foundational assumption of a biblical worldview that this world is moving toward some fundamental transformation. Therefore, history has direction and purpose. We are not just aimlessly adrift in the cosmos, but we are moving toward the new city, we are moving from the harlot to the bride.

Not on the wings of human progress,
not on the efforts of the good and righteous,
nor on the back of reason and technology,
but by God's sovereign hand…

Our text this morning proclaims that by some radical, gracious action God will make his dwelling with humanity, creation will be made new, and *shalom* will hold for eternity. And what we once saw dimly, we will see face to face. Where we once were distant, we will be intimate. And we who once were no people will be the people of the bride.

Neil Plantinga puts it this way:

> *We do not go to heaven; heaven comes to us. In a vision lovely enough to break a person's heart, John shows us what God showed him, that up ahead of us, after centuries*

> *of tribal feuds and racial arrogance, after centuries of xenophobic snapping at each other, after we humans have silted history full of the debris of our antagonisms – after all that, the city of God will descend to us, and God will dwell with us, and, once more, God will make all things new.*

I don't know a more profound hope or a more beautiful picture.

Therefore, let us invest ourselves in city building, for we don't go from garden to garden, as if what we do doesn't matter, but we go from garden to city, where human enterprise is somehow folded into, or part of, God's final purpose for creation. The city of God. A city to fall in love with…

Amen.

REFLECTIONS

REFLECTIONS

I took Dr. Stewart's instructions as divine guidance, and twenty years later the remaining task is to assess what difference it made. Does preaching make any difference?

> Hope grew and Hope shrank. We had a slew of babies and grieved the deaths of the generation that started Hope. We weathered the pandemic and planted a new church in the city – Grace in Garfield Park. We married and buried; we baptized and blessed. We reconfigured the sanctuary and built an addition. We marked liturgical seasons, the choir thrived, and we blended all manner of ages, voices, and musical styles in worship. We paid off our mortgage – twice. We settled refugee families. We watched loved ones move to west Michigan and we welcomed new friends. We sought to love God and love neighbor, to serve God and serve neighbor. We celebrated our 60th anniversary. We studied the Bible. We, we, we…

It's been an amazing, colorful, abundant twenty years.
We've been richly blessed.
Thanks be to God.

But I don't know what can be credited to preaching. Congregational life is complex and multi-faceted. Preaching is only one facet. Even in worship, preaching is but one part of a larger whole. I don't have any way to measure the difference...

> However, I can give an accounting of what I've learned. Rather than trying to assess any difference, maybe there's value in reflecting on the lessons learned in the process. Therefore, I'm taking the liberty to change the assignment: What did I learn about preaching while preaching at Hope?

What follows are a series of impressions and observations that are uniquely mine. One wonders why I didn't work out these issues in therapy, and this may all seem too self-serving or in defense of my eccentricities, but these are lessons from the lived experience of preaching.

> I'm not trying to break new homiletical or theological ground.
> I don't think for a minute that my experience is transferable.
> I'm not offering a guide for others.
> These observations are a capstone or a way to close this chapter.
> They're the reflections of a restless practitioner.
> Maybe this is the research thesis that never got written at Princeton.

WONDER

I was convinced that if I ever served a church as a preacher, I would kill the church within a few months. I was bound up with fear that I would run out of material and after a handful of sermons I wouldn't have anything to say. My paucity of insight would be revealed, the shallow waters of my soul exposed, and people would leave the church in droves.

But one Saturday in Schenectady, in the quiet of my study,

I stumbled across a phrase in the book of Isaiah that I'd never seen before. It was sublime, surprising, and lyrical. Its image tickled my imagination and its beauty pulled me upright. It was as if a window had been pushed open. Something breathed in me and I thought, *I can dig around in scripture for the rest of my life and always find the soil rich and fertile.* I can turn these texts over and over and over and

never run out of material,
never run out of mystery,
never run out of meaning.

Now that may not seem like much of a breakthrough, but it was an epiphany that gave me the courage to consider a call to Hope Church – that and a few years of therapy. That moment in Schenectady has taken on a mythic quality in my life. I think of it as being overwhelmed by the prospect of God speaking in the beauty, complexity, nuance, and mystery of scripture. It was wonderfully freeing. It wasn't about the material I brought to scripture; it was about listening for God's voice to emerge in scripture.

That was about 22 years ago, and I continue to take delight in the prospect of digging around in scripture. Not because of any fixed confidence about the nature of the Bible, or because I particularly like the spade work, but because again and again I find there

honest stories of what it means to be human,
windows into the nature of God,
ankle-breaking-twists that turn common readings on their heads,
nagging problems,
the breath of an abundant albeit messy life,
and the good news of God in Christ.

It seems to me, one sustaining gift in preaching is wonder. Or what Abraham Joshua Heschel describes as awe. In his words:

> *Forfeit your sense of awe, let your conceit diminish your ability to revere, and the universe becomes a marketplace for you. The loss of awe is the great block to insight. A return to reverence is the first prerequisite for a revival of wisdom, for the discovery of the world as an allusion to God. Wisdom comes from awe rather than shrewdness. It is evoked not by calculation but in moments of being in rapport with the mystery of reality. The greatest insights happen to us in moments of awe.... They who sense the wonder share in the wonder...*

Heschel is writing about creation, but the same is true for me about scripture. I've learned that preaching requires of me a willingness to wonder, wrestle, and wait for something to emerge. It doesn't always happen. It's hard to sustain wonder when you're cycling through the same texts, the same seasons, and the same stories. (As it turns out, Jesus is raised from the dead every Easter.) And, there's no way to continually stoke the fires of wonder when you're slogging through committee meetings and administrative minutia – even when those things are a welcome respite from the relentless pace of preaching.

But, without sounding like a pious-ass, I'm seeking after wonder with each text. I'm still astonished by the claims of scripture and the possibility that they're true. Therefore, when I turn to a text, one of the first tasks for me is to be open to its claims, to its absurdity, to its mystery, and to the wonder that I can't seem to shake.

If I've learned anything in this preaching project it's this: trust the text. Trust the text. Trust the text. My primary responsibility is to engage this ancient text and then get out of the way that others might listen for the voice of God - even when I don't have it figured out. Even when I'm still wondering, doubting, and wrestling with God. My patron saint is Jacob.

WRESTLING

For as long as I can remember, faith has been a struggle. Not unlike Jacob, my seminal experience is wrestling with God. I'm plagued with always being uneasy, unsettled, and unsure.

I've lived every one of my 63 years in the bosom of the church. I've opened heart, soul, and mind to God in Christ, and yet I can't seem to shut off the questions or stop seeing the shadows. I'm stuck with struggle – perplexed and barely hanging on. Sometimes the faith of my father and my friends was the only thing that kept me from abandoning the whole business. But as Christian Wyman writes (quoting Bonhoeffer and Augustine):

> *You must not swerve from the engagements God offers you. These will occur in the most unlikely places, and with people from whom your first instinct may be aversion. Dietrich Bonhoeffer says that Christ is always stronger in our brother's heart than in our own, which is to say, first, that we depend on others for our faith, and second, that the love of Christ is not something you can ever hoard. Human love catalyzes the love of Christ. And this explains why that love seems at once so forceful and so fugitive, and why, "while we may speak of this, and yearn toward it," as Augustine says, "we barely touch it in the quick shudder of the heart."*

All of this is to admit that while I don't know God as my mate, I've known the God of scripture as my wrestling partner. That struggle has its own intimacy, and it fosters a kind of identity, but it doesn't let one walk with confidence. It leaves me with a limp. It's what one preacher calls "the hermeneutic of the hip." And while it's not a spiritual disposition that I'd recommend, it is a way of reading scripture and being in relationship with God.

Phyllis Trible puts it this way:

> *Jacob's defiant words to the stranger I take as a challenge to the Bible itself: "I will not let you go unless you bless me." I will not let go of the book unless it blesses me. I will struggle with it. I will not turn it over to my enemies that it curse me. Neither will I turn it over to friends who wish to curse it. No, over against the cursing from either Bible-thumpers or Bible-bashers, I shall hold fast for blessing. But I am under no illusion that blessing, if it comes, will be on my terms – that I will not be changed in the process.*

Preaching, for me, is wrestling with the staggering implications of the incarnation, the resurrection, the possibility that the very Spirit of God dwells within our bodies, and the hope that the long arc of history does in fact end in *shalom*. And on and on and on. While I can't seem to settle into the interpretations of my liberal friends, I also choke on evangelical certainty. So, I'm left with a wrestling wonder.

We all come at scripture differently. Thanks be to God. What a sorry situation if we all came at it the same way. I only know to come at scripture and preaching with a wrestling wonder. For some, this disqualifies me immediately. For others, it feels like fresh air. I'm profoundly grateful that Hope Church welcomed and tolerated my limp. And I continue to be surprised that God uses it to sustain congregational life and announce good news.

THIRD EYE

In *Comedians in Cars Getting Coffee*, Jerry Seinfeld drives an exotic car to pick up a comedian. They drive around talking about comedy and then continue their conversation over a cup of coffee. That's it. Each episode is about 15 minutes long, and I find them fascinating.

In one episode set in Chicago, Jerry picks up comedian and talk-show host Steve Harvey in a 1957 black Chevy Bel Air Convertible with red and silver interior and a big rumbling V8. They drive around the city and end up having coffee at Manny's Delicatessen and Cafeteria on South Jefferson.

When they sit down over coffee, Jerry asks whether or not comedy can be taught. "Is it teachable?" Steve Harvey shakes his head and says,

> *Nah, man. If you explain it to them, it will make no sense. This is the most senseless profession on earth. I was born with this eyeball that sees everything different. Tragedy strikes. I got news for you. We have the jokes that night. Now we know that we can't bring them to the public yet, 'cause we'll get hammered. But in a room alone when it's just us, we have the jokes already. Listen to me, man, comedy is the one profession that's nontransferable. Comedians can become great actors, but actors can't become great comedians…*

He pointed at the center of his forehead and said, "I was born with this eyeball that sees everything different." Without that third eye that

sees the world slant,
sees the absurdity,
sees the incongruity,
sees the inappropriate,
sees the illogical,
sees the impossible,
there's no comedy.

That extra eye is also a curse. Many comedians are angst-ridden-wrecks who carry a lot of pain, but from there they see that things don't add up, and thus the jokes. You can't teach that.

I've wondered the same about preaching.

For some, preaching appears to be a science. I know wonderfully gifted preachers who exegete with precision and confessional clarity. They approach their work with great confidence in their scholarship, their theological heritage, and their expectations about scripture. They see things so clearly. Certain of their orthodoxy, they preach with great authority. I envy their aplomb. I envy how scripture works in their lives...

> But it doesn't work that way for me. I'm stuck with a third eye. I tend to see a question, a back door, a broken wing, or an expression of grace that extends beyond the boundaries. I tend to see what doesn't fit. I don't have the disposition or gifts of a scholar. (I grew up with a scholar. I know what I'm not.) Neither do I have a pure-hearted passion for spiritual matters or the things of God. I'm usually in the messy-muddled-middle. Not unlike the lukewarm water

> that gets spit out. Not Christian enough for the church, too Christian for the world. Throw in my attention deficit issues and I see the world through a cloudy, twitchy, lazy third eye.

That's both a gift and a curse. I know preaching to be more art than science, more creative than fixed, more question than certainty, more third eye than 20/20 vision. It's not that I have things figured out or that I'm seeing things rightly. It's not that I'm always trolling for sermon illustrations, but there's usually that nagging third eye with some theological image or implication disrupting my vision.

It probably serves me well as a preacher.
But a limp and a third eye?
I sound like a monster.

VOICE

My father was a history professor who left a tenured position at a major university to teach at a small, Christian, liberal arts college on the windswept tundra of northwest Iowa. He took a pay cut of more than a half in order to work at the intersection of faith and learning. He never looked back. He loved the interdisciplinary pursuit of truth in light of the gospel of grace in Jesus Christ.

I pushed back. Always. I didn't push against the move to Iowa, I pushed against my father's faith and his inability to understand or approve of the shallow waters of my adolescent life. He swam in deeper waters.

My father was always giving me books to read. When I asked a question, the answer often came with a book recommendation. Therefore, in high school I was reading Thomas Merton, *Zen and the Art of Motorcycle Maintenance*, John Howard Yoder's *Politics of Jesus*, Martin Luther King Jr., *The Post American*, etc. My father's faith was in the warp, woof, and water of my childhood. It was never a showy piety, never put on, and never set aside. It was oppressive, life-giving, and definitive.

While in my early twenties, I served an internship as the live-in manager of a house for men. It was Roseland Christian Ministries' first effort at providing shelter for the homeless – many of whom had addiction and mental health issues. It was a difficult living situation, and I wrote to my folks about my experience. This is part of what my father sent in response:

> *I do know that upholding the name of Christ and working to strengthen the church is finally all that is ultimately worthwhile. You are doing that as well as you can in a very difficult set of circumstances. Sin and social evil are somehow, in ways we may never know in this life, overcome as Christians suffer with and for Christ. It is not something we can manipulate into happening but God promises to work through us in our weakness. He works through our dying but he brings resurrection, as he promised. Our prayer is that you in your situation will have faith to live by that reality and that we in our situation will have the same confidence in the Lord.*
>
> *That sounds perhaps like pious rhetoric - I hope not. My sense of what it means to be a Christian seems to grow simpler all the time – what matters is God's way of overcoming evil; baptism, the Lord's supper, congregational*

fellowship, Bible study, all relate to that. Overcoming evil, meeting abundant sin with more abundant grace, is what the cross of Christ is all about. As the basis of our confidence in God's love for us and as the pattern for our lives in his will, it is what finally matters in the Christian life.

Keep up the writing, Roger; it is a good discipline for you, you have a flair for it, and it can help you sort out your thoughts and find some level of clarity in the confusion around us.

Beautiful.
Prophetic.
And imagine the pressure.

In finding my voice as a preacher, there's always been two realities in my heart and mind. There's my father's faith and its intellectual integrity; and there's my secular-spiritual-but-not-religious friends. I love them both. They're both looking over my shoulder. They're both listening.

I'm not defending one to the other.
I'm not trying to convert one to the other.
But I'm always mindful of both.
I'm trying to explain myself to both.
I'm trying to be faithful to the text for the sake of both.
I'm probably looking for the blessing of both.

Forty years after that letter from my father, and twenty years into this preaching assignment, I'm aware that I probably missed both. I'm not scholarly enough; I'm not secular enough. I'm not spiritual enough; I'm not worldly enough. It's that muddled-middle thing…

> There are families who left Hope over human sexuality issues who found spiritual renewal in the authoritative expository preaching of others. And I know that friends who are outside of the Christian tradition listen to or read my sermons and are dismissive when "there's too much Bible." I didn't aim for either and I missed both.

However, I didn't know how to do anything other than be honest with my longing for faith and my experience as the son of a Christian college professor. I've tried to be authentically me – straddling both worlds. I have no misgivings that my voice works for everyone. I know that my preaching is an acquired taste. A gentleman on a Search Committee from another church memorably said, "You know there are only a couple churches that would take you..."

But as Frederick Buechner writes:

> *At its heart most theology, like most fiction, is essentially autobiography. Aquinas, Calvin, Barth, Tillich, working out their systems in their own ways and in their own language, are all telling us the stories of their lives, and if you press them far enough, even at their most cerebral and forbidding, you find an experience of flesh and blood, a human face smiling or frowning or weeping or covering its eyes before something that happened once.*

All preaching is shaped by culture and experience, and it comes through an autobiographical lens. Therefore, I'm not suggesting that my voice is especially unique, but I've learned to accept that my preaching is shaped by my history. As Rachel Held Evans puts it, "My interpretation can only be as inerrant as I am, and that's good to keep in mind." I've learned that all I can offer is my peculiar lens. And then try to get out of the way that scripture can be heard, through my voice…

Again, this admission lets the orthodox dismiss me with cause. They can trot out evidence of post-modern relativism, a lack of confessional clarity, and being too swayed by the world. I feel no compulsion to defend myself. I don't need their sympathy or their approval. At this point, after spending the better part of my adult life doing this work, I'm weary of my faith being suspect and failing to meet the standards of a particular church culture.

I think it would be helpful if others recognized the determinative impact of experience, culture, and disposition. We're all doing the best we can with the material we've been given…

WRITING

I have a recurring nightmare.

> I'm supposed to speak somewhere – a church, a high school assembly, a chapel – but I don't have my manuscript. I can't get at it, the service has started, chaos is bubbling up, and I'm panicked. In some versions of this dream, I'm scrabbling around but not making any progress. In other versions, I'm standing in front of a crowd blah, blah, blah, blah, blah-ing about God and no one is listening. The nightmare is never resolved. I awake anxious, disoriented, and then gradually relieved when it dawns on me that it's only a dream. Again.

I don't know if that nightmare speaks of my need for control or my aversion to blathering on in god-talky cliches, but I do know that it points toward how essential writing manuscripts has become in my work as a preacher.

In some ways it's pragmatic. I don't have the confidence, quick wit, or charisma to speak extemporaneously with little more than an outline. Others have that gift.

In some ways it's protective. When I go off script it's typically to be smart-alecky. I'm usually looking for a laugh or seeking affirmation. Manuscript writing helps me limit those impulses.

And, in some ways, it's about precision. Writing helps with clarity. It helps me restrain extravagance, exaggeration, and Christian-speak. It helps me get to the heart of things.

The beginning point, every week, is scripture. People don't come to Hope for political discourse or five keys to a healthy marriage. They come to hear a word from scripture. Therefore, I start with a text – selected by the Revised Common Lectionary.

And yet there's always that blank page. There's the call to engage the text, and there's the challenge to unfold the text for others, but there's always the requirement to write something…

In my best moments, something in the text will hook me. In the reading, studying, and scouring of resources, something will tap into my curiosity and surprise or move me. Or I'll see something that troubles, that I can't swallow, or that makes me wonder. That's usually the entry point. If it sparks my interest, it will spark others' interest. If it breaks through my busyness and banality, it will do the same for others. That's where I try to start. In *Bird by Bird: Some Instructions on Writing and Life*, Anne LaMott identifies that beginning place.

> *If something inside of you is real, we will probably find it interesting, and it will probably be universal. So you must risk placing real emotion at the center of your work. Write straight into the emotional center of things. Write toward vulnerability. Risk being unliked. Tell the truth as you understand it. If you're a writer you have a moral obligation to do this. And it is a revolutionary act—truth is always subversive.*

That's a grandiose god-sized hope for weekly sermonizing. And for about four days of each week, that hope bubbles within me. I'm turning the text over and over. I'm thinking about stories and images. I'm living with the questions. I'm reading commentaries, other sermons, and running down rabbit trails. In my hopeful heart it still might be a great sermon, but I haven't written word one. There's still the blank page.

I put off writing for as long as I can because once I start writing, then all my limps and demons are on display. Once I start, I'm writing to meet a deadline and the air of my inflated hopes has long since sputtered out.

> I don't enjoy writing. There can be joy in a turn of phrase, but mostly it's a battle with ADD and the effort to write something faithful and honest about the text. Self-doubt and distractions get the better of me. I'm mindful of the others looking over my shoulder. It's a stilted, slow process. Eventually I'm just trying to fill the page and meet the deadline.

I know that for many, manuscripts limit the movement of the Spirit during the preaching moment. Manuscripts mitigate against getting caught up and carried away. Carefully curated words block the Spirit. They make preaching little more than a pencil-necked-book-report…

> But I've come to believe that if the Spirit is active in the preaching, the Spirit is also active in the writing. I write for clarity and to clear out as much clutter as I can. Are those not also concerns of the Spirit? Writing helps me hone in on the text, and that seems of the Spirit. I've learned not to limit the activity of the Spirit to preaching but to cherish the Spirit in the writing.

Barbara Brown Taylor is encouraging.

> *The effort to untangle the human words from the divine seems not only futile to me but also unnecessary, since God works with what is. God uses whatever is usable in a life, both to speak and to act, and those who insist on fireworks in the sky may miss the electricity that sparks the human heart.*

At the height of the Covid pandemic, Hope worshipped in the parking lot. We got a sound system, hooked up an electric piano, and encouraged folks to bring blankets and beach chairs. It was fun and beautiful in its own way.

In planning for those parking lot services, Erin Pacheco (Hope's Worship Arts Director) said that I needed to shorten my sermons. I was flabbergasted. No one had ever accused me of being long winded. Manuscripts curtail that sort of excess. Erin went on to explain that it would be hard for families to corral children in the parking lot and that the services needed a particular pacing. She was right.

Somewhere in that discussion, I got 1,600 words lodged in my head. My sermons should be 1,600 words. I'd never before paid attention to word counts. When you're trafficking in the Word of God there are no word limitations...

But that discussion prompted me to be more efficient. To write with an economy of language. To say things with as few words as possible. To clear out repetitive words and extra phrases. To ask of each sentence: How can it be written clearer, cleaner, and more concise? Without losing the text, can there be less language?

I like the challenge of making it fit 1,600 words.

I think it makes the sermons stronger.

I think it honors the listeners' time, spirit, and intellect.

I know it respects the rest of the service.

I shoot for 1,600 words.

COLLAGE

The Lilly Endowment has a remarkably generous history of funding projects that encourage congregational health. That commitment has given rise to all manner of support for pastors. Gather a group of pastors, and Lilly has the resources to enable your work together. I participated in a handful of Lilly-funded pastoral cohorts.

One of those groups was formed around "Preaching as Art." We met with a variety of artists, learned about their work and creative processes, and considered its application to preaching. (My young conservative friends are rolling their eyes right now. The church has squandered the pure preaching of the gospel for this sort of frivolity...)

One artist that this cohort met with was a printmaker. He had us make collages. On paper we laid out a variety of media, which was then run through an ink press, that in turn produced these delightful collage prints. We talked about the quality of the beginning materials, the contrasting colors, textures, and shapes that made up the collage, and then the surprise of the finished print.

I think of preaching as collage making.

> You start with disparate materials: Scripture, story, historical insight and commentary, experience, research, existential angst, novels, movies, and music. You use the best raw material that you can find. You arrange the pieces in some coherent-contrasting-colorful fashion. You pray and ponder. You run it through the writing press. And at the end there is something new,
>
> > something that you didn't see at the beginning,
> > something that's shaped by personality and process,
> > something that still bears the imprints of the beginning materials but is distinct and used of the Spirit.

That's to say that there's little original in sermon creation. Each sermon is a unique arrangement and an original collage, but the parts and pieces are the writing, work, and insight of others. Each sermon is the result of a creative process and the work of the Spirit, but the sermon itself is derivative. Sermons are constructed on the work and wisdom of others.

That reality makes plagiarism a constant danger. It's hard to read the writing of others and not bear their imprint. You can't break up a sermon by always noting and quoting others, but it's hard to write without influence and impression.

I try to give credit. I try to acknowledge when flow and

organization were shaped by others. I try to close the books, websites, and preaching resources and write what's left in my head. But what's in my head was put there by others…

The boundaries were fuzzy along the way.
I'm sure I crossed the line on occasion.
I found the collage metaphor to be really helpful.
I'm a collage maker.

CONVERSATION

The Cathedral Basilica of Saint Louis houses the largest collection of mosaics in the world. Work began on these mosaics in 1912, and they weren't completed until 1988. The images were created out of 41 million pieces of glass in eight thousand different shades of color. Each piece of colored glass is gold leafed on the underside and when set in cement by the artisan, they are arbitrarily tilted, creating an uneven surface. Therefore, when they catch light, they reflect an ever changing, glimmering kaleidoscope of color. The mosaic is always different, always dancing, always reflecting a unique shade of light.

Not unlike the Basilica mosaics, I've come to think of preaching as a conversation of light.

The source of light is the gospel of grace in Jesus Christ;
as that light is expressed in scripture and sermon,
it glimmers in all sorts of places and at all sorts of angles.
It's mirrored, bent, refracted, deflected, and muted.
It bounces off and overlaps.
It enhances and clashes and changes and illuminates
and moves…
Like a giant conversation of light.

Still with me?

This metaphor falls apart eventually, but there are a couple things I've learned to be true.

Scripture itself is a conversation of light.

> Scripture doesn't speak with one voice. Scripture is a raucous conversation. There's disagreement, conflict, correction, growth, and change. There are different genres, different voices, different perspectives, and different angles of light. And that cacophony of light ultimately shines in Jesus. Only to then splinter and fracture to illumine the mystery of Jesus: who he is, what he accomplished, what that means, and how then we might live in response to the "Light of the World."

Preaching is part of that conversation of light.

> Every preaching surface is uneven. As it reflects gospel light there's some flaw or finite quality. And yet, the light still shines. It still illumines. The full light can't be contained in any single sermon or any single preacher. We're all tilted pieces of glass. We all reflect the light at a unique angle. We all reflect the light slant.

Therefore, to mix metaphors, I don't have to hit a towering homerun or cover all the gospel bases with each sermon. I only need to be faithful to each particular text and to that particular ray of light. There's a much larger mosaic shining a gospel light.

This conversation of light is also the long, complicated, dynamic, conflict-ridden, life-giving, on-going conversation between preacher and congregation. It's a conversation for which the preacher is only a catalyst.

> There will be sermons that people don't like because there's too much glare, or not much glimmer, or they're a refracted mess. And there will be sermons that are sublime – just the light that some need. But at their best, sermons invite a continued exchange, a back-and-forth, even a twenty-year conversation.

I've learned to not obsess over a particular sermon's success or failure. They're just one piece of glass, one ray of light, and one more voice in an ongoing conversation. There's another sermon in a week. Individual sermons might flash or fizzle, but I've learned that what matters is sustaining the long conversation of light between scripture, Spirit, and congregation.

I'll never get my part in that conversation fully right. I need the corrective light of others, even as they might need mine. There's an open-ended quality to this conversation. But I've come to wonder if the only way to assess this unfinished conversation of light is by how we love God and love neighbor. Does preaching move us to love God and others?

Barbara Brown Taylor puts it this way:

> *I know that the Bible is a special kind of book, but I find it seductive as any other. If I am not careful, I can begin to mistake the words on the pages for the realities they describe. I can begin to love the dried ink marks on the page more than I love the encounters that gave rise to them. If I am not careful, I can decide that I am really much happier reading my Bible than I am entering into what God is doing in my own time and place, since shutting the book to go outside will involve the very great risk of taking part in stories that are still taking shape.*

> *Neither I nor anybody else knows how those stories will turn out, since at this point there is more blood than ink. The whole purpose of the Bible, it seems to me, is to convince people to set the written word down in order to become living words in the world for God's sake. For me, this willing conversion of ink back to blood is the full substance of faith.*

PHYSICAL

There's a generation of Western Theological Seminary students who memorize scripture. In preparation for preaching, they commit the biblical text to memory. They get the words in mind, spirit, and body. They live with the passage. They make it part of themselves. And then come Sunday morning, before the sermon, they recite the text with an ease of expression and emphasis.

The memorization of scripture is neither a discipline nor a spiritual gift in my arsenal. I went to Western at a different time and had different professors. I never had the preaching professor who promoted memorization. But I understand the need to get the text into mind, spirit, and body.

Typically, I wait until Tuesday morning to read the passage upon which the sermon will be based. Months ahead of time, I determined a preaching path, but I don't look at the sermon text until the week in which it will be preached. Because once I do, it takes up residence.

I do the required steps of reading and study. I look at different translations, consult commentaries, and check websites offering preaching prompts. I start to chase where my curiosity leads.

I look for what God is doing in the text. I begin to wonder what image, story, song, quote, or line will get me started or serve as a hook.

> But mostly I live with the text in my mind, spirit, and body. It's always there. It's not memorized, but I'm always thinking about it in some fashion – when I'm eating, awake in the middle of the night, aimlessly careening around the internet, or out for dinner with friends. It's always distracting. It's always on my mind and in my body.

On Friday or Saturday, I start to write. Intermittently, restlessly, I'm writing and rewriting until Sunday morning when I print it, preach it, and let it go. That process hasn't changed in twenty years, but I've learned two things.

One, I try to ride, run, or swim every day. I try to go longer on Saturdays. And almost without exception while I'm on the road or in the water there will be a sermon reconfiguration. A log jam will break,

a new angle will arise,
a new phrasing will emerge,
or a new insight will dawn.

I could sit for hours at my desk, laboring over my laptop, and never get to the same place. Stepping away, being outside, breathing and moving, creates space to listen differently. Things get clearer or there's a creative break-through. I don't know how it works. I'd like to credit the Holy Spirit. I know that it's physical. It has something to do with scripture in my body.

Two, I've always been a little weepy. I think it's genetic. My grandfather, uncles, and father were known to tear up when offering a prayer at the Thanksgiving table. And, on occasion, I'll push back a tear and try to not blubber while preaching. It still surprises, and I wish it didn't happen, but I think it has to do with what has been bottled up in my body all week. And then a line, a lyric, or a reference to a loved one is spoken, and tears leak out. Some beauty, some brokenness, or some deep longing for God will get the best of me. Maybe its triggered by anxiety, lack of sleep, or a genetic twig, but whatever it is, it's expressed in my body. Even if it's spiritual, it finds a physical expression.

Preaching is a physical act. The text, the study, the wondering, the praying, the writing, the preaching all comes through my body. It's affected by sleep, health, aging, and trauma. It's shaped by feeling, disposition, depression, joy, and ADD…

> That may seem obvious and not worth mentioning. Listening is a physical act. We encounter sermons in our bodies – in church, on YouTube, by podcast, and in books. But I've also learned that there's a physical expression or experience to preaching.

Throughout the week the words of scripture are dwelling in my body, and on Sunday they'll come out through my body – with all its quirks, gifts, and flaws. Preaching isn't solely an intellectual or spiritual endeavor; it affects our bodies. Twenty years ago, I didn't know that as clearly as I know it now.

Stanley Hauerwas writes that Christianity

> *is not a set of beliefs or doctrines one believes in order to be a Christian, but rather Christianity is to have one's body shaped, one's habits determined, in such a way that the worship of God is unavoidable.*

Creation, sin, incarnation, resurrection, and the hope of a coming *shalom* are all embodied realities. If I developed any manner of theology over the years it's the earthiness of goodness, guilt, grace, gratitude, and glory. I'm not inclined to write more about that here. I'm simply mindful of how preaching is also a uniquely physical expression of faith.

TRAUMA

Everyone has a story. Everyone has a story of brokenness, grief, or difficulty. If they don't now – they will. For some that story includes unspeakable abuse or horror. For some that story includes trauma. My story is one of trauma.

> While in my early twenties, my father was murdered a few feet away from me. While in my early sixties, I was cycling and was hit by a car. In both experiences there was no preparation or slow-dawning-awareness. In the matter of a few minutes or a split second – everything changed. And we (my family and I) were left to weave the trauma and loss into our lives.

If preaching comes through our voices, through experience and culture, through our bodies, and through our stories – then preaching, for me, also comes through trauma. My preaching has been shaped by trauma.

Very early on, I decided to exercise restraint in telling the story of my father's murder. I didn't want to commodify it or be identified by it. I didn't want to wear it as a badge or let it overshadow my work or responsibilities. It felt holy – telling it too often or too easily cheapened or chipped away at it.

> Therefore, I was very judicious how and when I shared the story. For a long while, as a high school teacher, I only told

> it once a year. At the ten-year anniversary I wrote about it. But mostly I refrained from telling it or talking about it. While preaching at Hope, I would go for months or years without mentioning it in sermons.

I'm not sure that's admirable. It was still impacting how I experienced the gospel. It was still seeping into what I wrote. But preaching didn't seem to be the place to work through the grief or develop a theology in which to hold the trauma. I think I'm trying to do something similar after being hit by the car. The accident is more recent, and I've been a little looser about it, but I reference that experience cautiously as well.

From my perch on Sunday mornings, it's impossible not to be mindful of the holy stories that reside in the Hope congregation. I know that I'm preaching to those who have buried children, struggled with infertility, and been abused. I know that there are listeners living with grief, trauma, depression, addiction, and all manner of struggle. Therefore, I'm not quick to announce what God is doing in our lives. I'm less inclined to suggest answers. Preaching, in part, is learning to sit with those who are longing for God.

A friend is fond of saying that preachers shouldn't preach until they're in their forties or they've had their heart broken. I checked both boxes.

> I'm not suggesting that my friend is right. There are fine preachers in their twenties and thirties. But there's an empathy, a measure of humility, and a longing for mercy that's rooted in loss and not systematic theology. Aging, brokenness, and sanctification can give one pause before proclaiming the Word of God. At least that's been true for me...

Again, I know that for many this observation immediately disqualifies me. Their confidence is in their confession about the nature of scripture and not human experience. I probably give too much credence to experience and these reflections will be used in preaching classes about the dangers of straying from confessional standards about the Bible.

However, I also know – deep in my body – that Christians are not somehow specially protected or particularly picked. Christ-followers suffer disease, are taken too early, know brokenness, and experience trauma.

> And while God is sovereign, there's no evidence that any of that comes from the hand of God. I don't think God is the author of the evil that happens in this world. I don't know when God is tinkering with the events of life so that we might learn a lesson or so that the details might adhere to some grand-cosmic-plan.

Trauma and preaching have taught me to confess both the sovereignty of God and that not all that happens is God's will. The best I can do is hold those two things loosely in faith.

After my father was murdered a seminary professor approached me. He'd buried a son who was in his early twenties. He rarely spoke about it, but in expressing concern for me he said,

> *If God were to write out the reasons why our son was taken, I would crumple it up and throw it back in God's face. There will never be reason enough.*

Of all the things that were said to me after my father's death, that's the only thing that I remember. There will never be reason enough.

Did I learn from trauma? Did it make me more compassionate and better able to identify with grief? Did it impact my work as a preacher?

Probably…

> But learning and being shaped by trauma doesn't mean that it was part of God's will. Maybe my heart is softer, maybe I know the long, jagged journey of grief, and maybe I have some idea of what it's like to be diminished, but there will never be reason enough. May we hold both sovereignty and brokenness tenderly and in tension.

That belief has shaped how I preached, sat with families in waiting rooms, and stood graveside. I'm sure that some wanted answers when all I could offer was the good news of Jesus and a longing for God.

LONGING

Sandi was the General Manager of our neighborhood brewpub. During her tenure, it was voted the Best Small Brewery in America at the Great American Beer Festival. It's a public house, a third place – after home and work – where community is shaped. A third place where black folks, white folks, Hispanics, Catholics, Jews, pagans, lesbians, evangelicals, the spiritual-but-not-religious, neighborhood kids, hipsters, and soccer moms rub shoulders.

During that season of life, I was immersed in bar culture and church culture. In listening to the stories in both communities, I heard the deep longing that's in all of us…

> There's a longing for healing, for wholeness, for mercy, for love to be embodied, for joy, and for this world to be put to

rights. That longing finds different expressions in pub and parish. There's all manner of ways that we seek to satisfy, deflect, or deny that existential reality, but underneath it all, the longing is the same.

Blaise Pascal and Saint Augustine name that longing as missing God. To paraphrase, we're all trying to fill the god-shaped hole in our hearts, or we're restless until we rest in God. And they're probably right. But I'm mindful of many who would take great offense at the diagnosis that they have a hole in their lives. In a multitude of ways, they're thriving and life feels full. To name their underlying restlessness and longing as the absence of God seems the height of hubris. There are all sorts of expressions of faith that fill those holes.

And yet, I kept hearing in the faithful and the unchurched, in the guy at the bar and the man in the pew, in the convicted and the searchers, some deep longing…

I've learned that part of preaching is listening for that longing in the text, in the lives of the listeners, and in my own heart. And then letting that longing find voice. It wasn't a rhetorical strategy. It was an authentic expression of my own longing for God.

Flannery O'Connor wrote to a struggling friend that faith requires the prayer of Peter, "Lord, I believe. Help my unbelief." She followed that encouragement with the observation that "in the life of a Christian, faith rises and falls like the tides of an invisible sea." And that even when we can't see it or feel it – faith is still there, "more valuable, more mysterious, altogether more immense than anything you can learn or decide…"

I've learned that faith fluctuates and that even when we're not focused on it, faith is still there. God's covenant in Christ is secure; it doesn't float on the tides of faith. And as I learned to give voice to a biblical faith, I was being formed by something larger, more mysterious, and more valuable than my own doubts and intellectual life. I did the best I could to be faithful to the biblical narrative.

Early on in my tenure at Hope I preached an Easter sermon entitled, *Myth, Metaphor, or Meaning.* It was terrible. I was trying to offer ways to think about the mystery of the resurrection and still land at a place of great faith. Did I mention it was terrible?

> After communion and a rousing rendition of the Hallelujah Chorus, one of Hope's saints pulled me aside to tell me that it was a fine sermon but that he didn't want to hear my questions and struggles on Easter morning. He wanted to hear the story of Jesus rising from the dead.

I took his counsel to heart.
I tried to preach an orthodox Christianity.
I didn't try to dismantle faith or deconstruct scripture.

My experience as a preacher was not shaped by a courageous faith or the confidence to chip away at orthodoxy. My experience as a preacher was defined by wrestling wonder and a desire to engage scripture. I don't think I preached my doubts or my wounds. I preached grace upon grace in Christ.

And yet, underneath all of that…
underneath the ebb and flow of faith,
underneath trying to proclaim this ancient text,
underneath the ongoing conversation with scripture,
Spirit, and congregation,

> underneath it all – for me – there was still a deep
> longing for God.

When I didn't have answers, I still longed for God. When there were barriers to belief, I still longed to believe. And most Mondays – when I was typically questioning my life choice as a preacher – I was still longing that somehow the claims of scripture were true.

> *Lord, I believe. Help my unbelief.*

Therefore, in preaching, I was trying to find the intersection between wonder and longing. And then invite others into that space to listen for God's voice. That's a tall order – even with the Spirit's help. It's way more than I was able to do. I don't want to give the impression that I routinely found that intersection. And yet, that's what I was trying to do. I was trying to engage scripture with wonder and be honest about the longing that won't let me rest.

Frederick Buechner famously wrote that

> *Whether your faith is that there is a God or that there is not a God, if you don't have any doubts, you are either kidding yourself or asleep. Doubts are the ants in the pants of faith. They keep it awake and moving.*

Living with scripture week in and week out and giving the better part of my life to proclaiming the good news of God in Christ helped keep my doubts at bay. But longing always animated my faith and stimulated my preaching. The ants in my pants kept me fidgety, restless, and honest.

And so, as I experience it, preaching is an act of desperation and affirmation.

I'm desperate to believe and remain tethered to faith and community. And I'm trying to affirm the mystery of God in Christ and the way of Jesus. I don't have other answers. There's not some other "world and life view" that I'm promoting. While I read across the theological spectrum, I'm not inclined to pull in a particular direction. I'm just trying to hold onto and be held by a robust Reformed understanding of God, Jesus, resurrection, atonement, soteriology, eschatology, Christology. All the ologies.

How people respond or how they experience belief hasn't been a high priority. I understand Hope to be a community of fellow wrestlers. Uniformity of thought, interpretation, or confessional detail rarely occurs to me. We're trying to keep a big tent. And I've tried to be mindful of that in preaching.

I'm not trying to convince anyone.
I'm not trying to offer an apologetic.
I'm trying to listen to scripture and invite others
into the same.

That's not to say that there isn't some desired outcome…

Loving God and neighbor, keeping the commandments, seeking first the Kingdom, following the way of Jesus, forgiving as we're forgiven, bearing the fruits of the Spirit, welcoming all, siding with the marginalized, telling the truth to God and one another.

Those are high goals and values. I hope my preaching encourages living a Kingdom ethic. Given the complexities of contemporary life, differing political philosophies, and the collateral damage of culture wars, I pray that my preaching helps Hope be the "Beloved Community."

But the nature of belief, how we understand faith, and how we live with our questions and our longings, all of that seems like part of our ongoing communal conversation. We listen and trust and long for God.

COMMUNITY

In response to the Covid pandemic, Hope ramped up its technology. We installed two unobtrusive cameras and developed a little sermon podcast. Post-pandemic, we now have faithful friends who tune-in from out-of-state and out-of-country. If we were better at self-promotion, we'd advertise our international media ministry.

When services were suspended, there was something intriguing about preaching in an empty sanctuary. It was just my voice and just what I wrote. I didn't have to make eye contact. I didn't have to notice the gentleman sleeping in the second row or wonder about the one in the back scrolling through his phone. It was church without people. Erin Pacheco handled music, and Schuyler Roozeboom handled technology. We were a merry little team, and it was fun for a few weeks.

Until it wasn't.

Preaching is a communal act. It's more than sharing biblical information or offering tips for living. It's more than the noodlings of a restless soul or the charisma of a skilled orator. Preaching is more than sermons.

Preaching lives, and moves, and has its being in community.
Peaching requires the participation of others.
Preaching takes a village.

I learned early on that I was one part of a larger whole. Good preaching required good music, accessible liturgy, and honest prayer.

"Liturgy" can be understood as "the work of the people." The whole community needs to play their role. Therefore, Hope invested in getting people of all ages and stages to lead in liturgy and music. We tried to develop and enhance the collective experience of worship with the collective gifts of the community. We tried to steer clear of worship as entertainment. We tried to involve the whole Hope family in the "work" of worship.

So, this little sermon collection needs a soundtrack. In this printed format, without music, these sermons stand naked and alone. They're unfinished without a hymn, song, or anthem of response. Pretty much every sermon I delivered over the last twenty years ended with music. What I didn't say, or what needed to be affirmed, celebrated, prayed, or pleaded was often in the music.

The communal nature of preaching saved me from myself. I was less inclined to get stuck in my own head or think that church growth or decline swung on my preaching. All I could do was my part. All I could offer was the best I could muster. I didn't feel the full burden. I shared the load with musicians, liturgists, the choir, those who led in prayer, and folks sitting in the sanctuary.

> Preaching is a fifty-fifty venture. Half of the experience hangs on the listeners' expectations, dispositions, and what they had for breakfast. We all have to play our parts…

Rachel Held Evans gets at it this way:

> *Christianity isn't meant to simply be believed; it's meant to be lived, shared, eaten, spoken, and enacted in the presence of other people. They reminded me that, try as I may, I can't be a Christian on my own. I need a community. I need the church.*
>
> *I often wonder if the role of the clergy in this age is not to dispense information or guard the prestige of their authority, but rather to go first, to volunteer the truth about their sins, their dreams, their failures, and their fears in order to free others to do the same. Such an approach may repel the masses looking for easy answers from flawless leaders, but I think it might make more disciples of Jesus, and I think it might make healthier, happier pastors. There is a difference, after all, between preaching success and preaching resurrection. Our path is the muddier one.*

I didn't set out to be a preacher. When I was in seminary, preaching seemed like the last place I'd land. I didn't want to "go first" with my sins, dreams, failures, and fears.

But as I was welcomed into the faith family at Roseland Christian Ministries, I was attracted to an embodied faith that was expressed in food, tears, laughter, preaching, music, and shared commitments. I lived in a community that was flawed and fallen (like every community) and yet was loving one another in what – to a young-middle-class-white-guy – seemed like difficult circumstances. Investing in that kind of community seemed like a worthwhile way to spend a life.

Therefore, while I don't know what difference preaching makes, I do know that whatever gifts I have are invested in sustaining community. Hope's communal DNA was set by the founding pastor and those who followed. I'm just trying to run my leg of the relay. And at some point, I'll pass on the baton.

The Hope family is scattered all over the city and suburbs. We represent all sorts of political positions and theological traditions. We're a volunteer organization, filled with flawed humans, who are trying to love God and love neighbor. While we face different issues than our brothers and sisters in Roseland, we're trying to do the same thing. We're trying to embody a gospel of grace in Jesus Christ.

I'm grateful for Hope's intergenerational community life.

My part has been to bear witness to God in scripture.

Not a bad way to spend a life.

LISTENING

After the Prayer for Illumination, and before I read scripture, I typically say, "Listen, then, for the voice of God."

We ask God to shine a light on our reading. In song, solo, silence, spoken word, or choral anthem we ask God to shape our hearts and lives by what we read and what we hear. And then before we listen as a community...

Listen, then, for the voice of God.

I don't know where I got that line, but I say it every week.

We follow the reading of scripture with this responsive line:

The Word of the Lord.
Thanks be to God.

I'm not making any claim about the Bible. I'm not announcing anything about the nature of scripture or sermon. Neither am I denying anything. I am simply inviting us to listen for God's voice. I'm inviting the Hope community into the shared experience of listening to the biblical text, to the sermon, and to the Spirit – for the voice of God.

That's to affirm that God is still speaking

That's to affirm that we have the capacity to hear God's voice.

That's to acknowledge that we can also miss God's voice.

There are all sorts of voices demanding our attention. Our lives are flooded with information, opinion, entertainment, story, outrage, and grievance – the tantalizing and the tawdry. Never before have there been so many voices paired with so much technology – all vying to be heard, liked, friended, bought, and loved. We live in a noisy world.

And yet, amidst all that racket, we gather in a modestly-sized church, on a nondescript corner, in an average Midwest suburb, that we might hear the voice of God.

Given all the other calls, we're trying to listen for God's call. Given the immediacy of texts, tweets, and TikTok, we're trying to listen to a collection of ancient manuscripts for the way and will of God. Given the distractions of the present, we're trying to attend to the God of covenant history.

That's a counter-cultural act. That cuts against the grain of a walk in the woods, brunch at the newest farm-to-table restaurant, or a quiet morning reading *The New York Times*. That's to choose an alternative to every other community that gathers on Sunday mornings to ride, run, surf, hunt, hike, do yoga, or tailgate. Gathering for worship means putting down our phones that we might listen for something that's beyond the flick of our fingers and the noise in our souls.

In biblical passage and spoken sermon we expect to hear God speak. That's an audacious, knee-buckling claim. As Annie Dillard reminds us:

> *Does anyone have the foggiest idea what sort of power we so blithely invoke? Or, as I suspect, does no one believe a word of it? The churches are children playing on the floor with their chemistry sets, mixing up a batch of TNT to kill a Sunday morning. It is madness to wear ladies' straw hats and velvet hats to church; we should all be wearing crash helmets. Ushers should issue life preservers and signal flares; they should lash us to our pews. For the sleeping god may wake someday and take offense, or the waking god may draw us out to where we can never return.*

But there we are, week after week.
There we are, year after year.

I've been privileged by profession, constitution, and family history to spend a lifetime trying to hear God in scripture. And while it's been an uneasy fit, twenty years later the best reason that I can think of for participating in church life is the expectation that together we would hear God's voice.

> Given all the other voices in our heads, we're trying to listen for an alternative, for something outside of us, for the Creator-Redeemer God. Given all the other gifts of church life – congregational singing, marking life's passages, a community of friends, seeking the good of others – the center is still the Word of God. And one way that we encounter the Word is in the words…

Yes, there are other places and other ways that God speaks.
Yes, we encounter God in the sacraments.
Yes, there are other ways to engage the God of scripture.
Yes, churches are broken bodies and fallen institutions.

But I'm still tethered to congregational worship and preaching as a way to hear God's voice. Given my limps and limitations, the call on my life has been to help a community listen for the voice of God. And in listening, to seek after the Kingdom.

At the end of a worship service in the fall of 2022, as I stood up to offer the benediction, a couple Elders walked forward to say something. They called Sandi up front (not her favorite thing), and with a generous gift and some kind words they recognized our twenty years at Hope. I was blindsided, awkward, and I hope I adequately expressed my deep gratitude.

One of the elders shared a lovely reflection on our life together and said that I pretty much have only three themes in every sermon: Grace. Grace. And. Grace.

Scott Hoezee summarizes it this way:

> *It is the overall arc of a given preacher's sermons that over time build up a kind of happy, gracious residue in people's souls.... Preachers who take care (as all preachers should) again and again to proclaim grace and hope and joy convey over time that grace and hope and joy are the main items of the faith. It's not about doom-and-gloom, hellfire-and-brimstone – not firstly and not at the end of the Gospel day. It's about noticing the marginalized, about forgiving each other again and again, about holding on to hope even when life's dodgiest and toughest questions*

are staring us right in the face. It's about resurrection and new beginnings and fresh hope all the time.

I don't really have anything other to offer.
Even at my most self-indulgent, I was trying to point to Jesus.
You are loved and accepted by God in Christ.
It's grace, all the way down.
Ours is only the gratitude.

That's what I've been trying to say – even in this little hodge-podge collection of observations. As one "bent and crippled by sin like all the rest of humanity" (Fleming Rutledge), I'm profoundly grateful for Hope Church and for twenty years together listening for the voice of God. Thank you.

ACKNOWLEDGMENTS

I'm grateful for Hope's sabbatical policy and that Hope's leadership kept encouraging me to take one. This self-published-project was the work of that sabbatical. In a variety of ways Jeff and Ginny Carpenter, Sally Larsen, Aron Reppmann, and Russ Hollender ensured that it would happen. Thank you.

There are many at Hope who have given wise counsel, offered encouragement, and helped navigate the journey. That list is too long to recount, but it surely includes Dave Larsen, Jack Hoekstra, Glenn Medema, Richard DeJong, Melissa Varghese, Gerrit Veenstra, Becky Starkenburg, and Chris Gabrielse.

This little sermon collection wouldn't have happened without Schuyler and Corenna Roozeboom. Their expertise and willingness to help was delightful and essential. They're delightful and essential. Steve Vryhof's supportive friendship and lots of breakfasts together kept this idea alive. Thank you.

A preacher staying in one place for 20 years is not uncommon, but it's almost unheard of to work with the same staff for that long. I'm profoundly grateful for Sharon Aardema, Marianne Lydon, Marjie Coleman, Dora Diephouse, Lynn Hollender, David and Beverly Baar, Jean Sinclair, Rita Hollender, Mary

Van Loh and Kate van den Brink. They each generously offer generous gifts. I'm grateful for our shared work, shared friendship, and shared commitment to Hope.

Erin Pacheco started as a college intern and eventually became Hope's Worship Arts Director. She's a wonderful musician, preacher, theologian, and church-planter. I think of her as a partner in ministry. I'm thankful for her investment in Hope.

22 years ago, I walked into David Olsen's office. I'm still there. I wouldn't have answered Hope's call and I wouldn't have lasted without David's work and wisdom. That's meant a lot of therapy and I'm not fixed yet, but I'm blessed to call him a friend.

I've got a band of brothers who have taken my phone calls and stuck with me: Bob Bast, Mitch Kinsinger, Harlan Van Oort, Taylor Holbrook, Jeff Munroe, Mark Kuiper, Joe Huizenga, and Jack Nikcevich. Thank you. "I'll keep movin' through the dark with you in my heart, my blood brother."

And finally, Sandi, Zach and Chelsea, Lauren and Mark, I couldn't be prouder or more grateful for you. I never dreamed I'd be so blessed. This slim volume is evidence of what I've been doing in my black chair. I hope it's meaningful for you and someday for Jack and Emma, but all these words are just religious rhetoric and a ridiculous racket without love. And, I love you.

ABOUT THE AUTHOR

Roger Nelson is husband to Sandi, father to Zach & Chelsea, Lauren & Mark, and grandfather to Jack & Emma. A graduate of Western Theological Seminary, he was a high school teacher and coach for ten years before working as a pastor. Currently he serves Hope Christian Reformed Church in the southwest suburbs of Chicago. A four-time Ironman, he's an avid runner, rider, and reader.

More sermons are available for listening on the
Spoken in Hope: Sermons from Hope CRC podcast.

CONTACT

Roger Nelson / Hope CRC
5825 151st Street, Oak Forest, IL 60452
rog@hope-crc.org

CPE / Hebrew

. Action - reflection - new action

(make mistakes)

. body . spirit

drawing, visual, art on hospital walls.

Made in United States
North Haven, CT
02 June 2023

37256184R00189